332.024 Dissinger,
DIS   Katherine.

Old, poor, alone,
and happy

Old, Poor, Alone, and Happy

Old, Poor, Alone, and Happy

How to Live Nicely on Nearly Nothing

Katherine Dissinger

Nelson-Hall nh Chicago

Library of Congress Cataloging in Publication Data

Dissinger, Katherine.
 Old, poor, alone, and happy.

 Includes index.
 1. Finance, Personal. 2. Aged women—Economic conditions. I. Title.
 HG179.D56   332'.024   79-23731
 ISBN 0-88229-629-9 (Cloth)
 ISBN 0-88229-752-X (Paper)

Manufactured in the United States of America

10   9   8   7   6   5   4   3   2   1

To the Ladies of the Landmark
who helped me write this book

Contents

1.

Introduction

This is a book for women who are old and poor and alone —and for those who will be someday. If you know how, you can live richly, fully, happily, even exuberantly and joyously, though old and poor and alone.

There are so many tragic old people fumbling about in abject poverty or shut up in nursing homes, living empty, lonely, meaningless lives because they didn't know how to cope; they didn't plan for the future and didn't prepare for it. This book tells how to develop coping techniques and skills, how to solve some of the problems peculiar to old age and poverty and aloneness. It is a practical book, and it works.

The golden years should be just that—golden. Old age should be a good time of life, even the best time. It is a matter of making wise decisions and wise choices, the right decisions and the right choices for you.

Many people seem to come smack up against old age as if it had crept over them without any warning at all. They are suddenly old and suddenly alone; they feel stupefied and

lost and hurt by the confrontation, unable to cope intelligently. They have made no preparations or plans; they have
planted no seeds and built no fences. Everyone ought to get
ready for old age because it is on the way. If you should live
so long, it will happen. To be ready for it is to win the battle.

Some of us retired with enough to live on, but, with continued inflation nipping away at our fixed retirement incomes,
many of us are now either living on the very fringes of poverty
or are right in the middle of it. In fact, some of us are floun-
dering in it, gut-poor. Times are not going to get any better
for us; they are going to get worse, and so we'd prepare for
them—or we should.

How to cope with poverty is one of our biggest problems.
That is what this book is mainly about—how to live nicely
on nearly nothing, how to get a lot of mileage out of a little
money, how to *enjoy* life on a little money, and how to cope
with the many problems that confront the aging poor.

At this stage of the game, it is not possible for most of
us to actually improve our financial situation to any great
extent. Nobody is going to drop a fortune into our laps. But
we can learn to cope with poverty creatively instead of grimly.
We can learn to live creatively and happily in it.

Even if you are presently living well above the poverty
level, some of the penny-pinching pointers should enable you
to save for something you really want in a hurry. It may not
be necessary to economize in all areas, but only in a few.

For years I was one of those who simply let life happen to
them. I didn't plan or shape it to my liking. I went blithely
along with whatever came, whatever life handed me. But
people who lead unplanned lives seldom get anywhere, because they don't know where they are going or even where
they want to go.

I changed all this when I retired. I systematically began doing all the things I'd always wanted to do, learning all the
things I'd always meant to learn, began to live creatively and

constructively. For the first time, I had a planned life, as organized as a street guide.

This is what makes a happy old age—planning for it, taking hold of life and shaping it to your liking. I had to learn to be old, poor, alone and happy, and so can everybody. There is no situation so overwhelming it cannot be coped with, no problem that does not have a solution.

My way won't necessarily be your way. But after reading this, you should be able to work out something that is exactly right for you. You, too, can make your old age a very happy time.

2.

Planning and Managing – Your Money and Your Life

Poor old ladies may be divided rather neatly into two categories—those who have only a little money, and those who have none at all. It is entirely possible to be old and alone and quite penniless through no fault of your own. If you fall into this latter category, the situation is not hopeless —there are ways of getting help and coping.

You Have a Little

Almost everyone who retires these days has a little something—Social Security, a pension, a little property, a few investments, or a savings account. Let's hope you have a little money to fall back on in case of emergency. Nothing gives one a sense of security like money in the bank; you don't need a lot if your monthly income is adequate to meet your needs, but you should have some, and the more the better, of course. Living from hand to mouth, wondering where you'll get your next meal, and worrying about where the next month's rent is coming from is enough to drive anyone to the tranquilizing pills.

An old friend of mine who can not or will not budget almost has a nervous breakdown when her Social Security check is late because she has nothing to live on while she waits for it to arrive. Budgeting and intelligent restraint would solve her problem.

What Are You Going to Do with the Little Money You Have?

First of all, you need a checking account. Keeping a large sum of money in your house or on your person is not smart or safe. But, before you open a checking account, look for a bank that does not charge you for the checks you write. It's attention to these small details that enables you to live nicely on nearly nothing. It is foolish to pay ten or fifteen cents every time you write a check. Often you will have to maintain a minimum balance in order to check free of charge, and this is good too. It makes you more wary of overspending. Some banks permit senior citizens to check free of charge without a minimum balance.

It's well to have your Social Security, pension, and retirement checks sent directly to the bank. There are forms to be filled out to enable you to do this. Having checks sent to the bank eliminates worrying about checks being stolen from the mailbox or going to the wrong address. Also, it saves you the trouble of going out to deposit the check each month.

Once you have an account, keep your check stubs diligently and accurately. When your checks and statement balance come from the bank every month, compare them with your check stubs to see that they tally. Always know to the dollar how much you have in your checking account.

Putting Your Money to Work for You

Maintaining more than a minimum balance in your checking account is not good money management. Savings accounts that draw interest should hold the surplus. Find a savings and loan institution that compounds interest daily. Savings and loan institutions usually pay a higher rate of interest than banks. Interest can be withdrawn every three months if desired. Even if the interest amounts to only five dollars, it pays to have your extra money in a savings account. The five dollars is enough for a play, a dinner with friends, or a little present for someone.

It is convenient to have one kind of account where you can deposit and withdraw at any time. This kind of account pays slightly less interest than some other kinds, but whenever you need extra money you can get it without any trouble at all.

The bulk of your savings, if you have more than a few thousand dollars, will draw more interest if placed in a certificate of deposit, usually about 7½ percent if left for four or five years. Unless you are an astute businesswoman—and you probably aren't or you wouldn't have ended up old and poor—this is a good, safe place for your money. However, there is a stiff penalty for withdrawing the principal before the time is up, so it is well to have enough in your first savings account to take care of any and all emergencies—a dental bill you couldn't budget for, new glasses, a trip you can't resist, a little loan to someone you love, or a replacement for some essential item. Though you should not touch the principal on a certificate of deposit, you can draw your interest every three months—nice fun money!

Inflation being what it is, you aren't making any money by putting your spare cash in a savings and loan association, but you aren't in danger of losing your whole pot either. And unless you are clever, you can! We all know old people who invested their money in some get-rich scheme—or even some more conventional ones—and lost everything they had.

Before depositing your money, compare interest rates. Find out if interest is compounded daily. Find out if the account is insured by the federal government. It should be—usually up to $40,000.

If you have more than $40,000 to be stashed away, you

need the advice of an investment counselor, not mine; and, if you are in that category, this book is not for you unless you are interested in leaving a legacy to your grandchildren and are willing to live frugally to do so.

If you need financial counseling, seek expert professional help. Do not depend on the advice of friends or relatives or somebody you met on the train. Under no circumstances should you turn your financial affairs over to anyone but a professional, and I would be leery of doing that.

Do not expect—or permit—your children to take over your financial affairs, no matter how expert or well-meaning they may be. Stay in charge and on top of your own affairs as long as you can; put your money to work for you; learn to handle your own business in an intelligent, efficient manner; and hang on to your own money.

Don't give it away to anyone—yet. Don't even loan it, except in very small amounts. Loaning large sums often creates ill feeling and tends to cool a warm relationship. I know a woman who loaned her only son almost all she had to buy a beautiful house, and now she is living in a furnished room and cooking on a hot plate. As long as you have control of your money, you have control of your life. Let go of it and you've lost both!

Making a Will—Getting Ready to Live

Making a will does not mean you are getting ready to die, but to live, free and unencumbered by fear and worry. We plan and prepare for the future, and thus we are free to devote ourselves to the present. That is why you must have a will. You should make a will no matter how little you have —it simplifies matters. Who is going to get the few thousand remaining in your bank account, the blue plate that belonged to Aunt Agatha, or the little diamond ring? With a will, you can leave them to someone who will enjoy them the most.

You should go to a lawyer and have him draw up your will; the little thing written in your own hand on a piece of violet notepaper will cause no end of confusion. If you don't know a lawyer or anyone who can recommend one, call the lawyer referral service listed in the phone book. They will usually recommend several young ones who need your business. When you call to make an appointment, ask about the charges for making a will so you will know what to expect, and shop around a bit—some charge less than others, and it doesn't take a Nobel Prize winner to draw up a will.

Put your copy of the will in a safe place with your other important papers and tell family and friends where they are.

Organizing Your Papers and Place— Getting Things in Order

While you are at it, it is well to get all your other papers in order, too, and neatly file them in a divided brown paper folder you can buy at the dime store, or better, in a little fireproof strongbox—receipts, copies of income tax forms, savings account books, bank statements, cancelled checks, correspondence you wish to keep, birth certificate, passport, warranties, and whatever else is important in the handling of your affairs and your business. Then you can put your hand on whatever you need in a moment. You don't have to spend hours looking for things and sorting through the stacks of miscellany some old ladies seem to collect.

Insurance

Health Insurance

When you don't have much money, or even if you do, adequate health insurance is essential. Everyone over sixty-five has Medicare, of course, but most of us feel the need for supplementary insurance to take care of expenses that Medicare doesn't cover. Look around very carefully to find health insurance that seems to best meet your particular needs and circumstances.

Buy health insurance the way you buy everything else, now that you have plenty of time—comparison shop. Find out what various companies offer and for what price. After evaluating all the information, make your decision as to the kind and amount of insurance you need. Some people will need and want more insurance than others, but be sure that what you have will take care of practically all medical expenses that Medicare doesn't. Otherwise, you may find all your emergency and fun money going to doctors and hospitals.

Other Insurance to Be Considered

Fire and theft insurance on household possessions does not seem to be considered essential by many older people living in rented apartments. Having insurance is no excuse for not locking and bolting your door and taking precautions to prevent fire and theft, but it does give one a sense of security. If you have many possessions of value, you probably do need fire and theft insurance.

If you decide to insure, itemize all your belongings and write down the year of purchase and the price paid. Go through the house and take pictures of your various possessions, have them developed, and file them with your policy.

Burial Insurance

Paid-up burial insurance is another thing many older people will want. Most burials are expensive these days, whether you want them that way or not. There are other alternatives, however. Cremation—having one's ashes scattered to the winds or over water—is usually less expensive than other forms of burial and one that some people find satisfying and beautiful.

A more altruistic solution and one that I find even more satisfying in that it costs nothing is to donate your body to a medical center for medical research and education. It is necessary to make prior preparation by writing to your state university medical center for forms which are to be filled out, witnessed, and signed by your next of kin. Upon receipt of the signed forms, the center will send you a card to carry in your wallet which begins, "In the event of my death. . . ."

Realistic Planning for the Future

In order to be prepared for all contingencies (such as the very end of the road), you need to ask yourself, What happens when I get so old I can no longer maintain myself in my own happy place, can no longer walk about, cook for myself and look after my own needs, or when I get so funny I forget to turn off the stove and can't find my shoes in the morning?

It's well to make plans before this happens. How about putting a little money aside each month to buy yourself into a retirement home for old ladies, with three meals a day furnished and a square little room with a single bed in it? A home like that is the best place for decrepit old ladies, the only place, in my opinion. Nobody should expect the family to take her in and look after her in her dotage.

So, I must plan my life and my spending so I will have money enough when I come close to the end of the road to get into one of these retirement homes. I investigate and compare while I can still get around. I find out how much I will have to pay to get in and how much the monthly fee will be. Would my retirement income cover it? Would there by any left over? There doesn't need to be much left over, for what does a decrepit old lady need but three meals a day and care? A trip to the doctor and a few clothes now and then. Everything else is provided.

You must *walk* into most of these retirement homes. So, when you feel yourself beginning to slip, you pay your money and wait until there's a vacancy and then move in. And you hope your timing will be right, soon enough—but not too soon.

If you don't quite make it, there will be a nursing home somewhere. I visited an old lady recently in one of these homes—one of the grimmer ones where people don't look like people any more—and she broke into her bitter tirade: "I never thought I'd end in a place like this."

But, I wanted to say: "Why didn't you? You should have." Because that's where many of us will end, and what's so bad about it? Especially if you've had a good and happy life up to then.

You have to be a realist to get along in this world. If you can face and accept the reality before it happens, then the actual happening comes as no surprise, no shock. You will have prepared yourself for what you are going to do, and you will know how to cope. Then you are ready to enjoy the life that's left you, without worry or fear.

Death: The Last Reality

Death is another thing that ought to be faced before it happens, so the idea won't be strange when it comes. Not dwelt upon, just faced. Death means different things to different people—the end for some, a beginning for others. When you get old, you get a new feeling about death.

Old ones who fear it, fear not death itself, I think, but confuse their fear with regret for a meaningless, futile existence; an unhappy looking back; and a wish that life could be redone. I believe that those who have lived richly and well do not fear death and do not dread it.

Death means different things to different people depending on the extent and intensity of their religious faith. How wonderful to be one of those with great and undiluted faith who can give up this life without a qualm and go calmly and confidently to their reward—I sometimes envy their serenity. But if you are one of those people, try not to let your faith lead to smugness towards those who lack your confidence.

I have alway liked new things, change, variety, new experiences, adventure, or a journey into unknown territory. I can think of death now as another adventure—the last long trip, the ultimate experience. Whatever else it is, death is that also. Not to be welcomed but not to be unduly delayed or dreaded either.

You Don't Have Anything at All

If you were unfortunate or unlucky and now find yourself in this situation, you must have help. Contrary to what some people believe, it is possible to live nicely on welfare. I know people who do, and I also know those who don't know how to spend their money to advantage or don't know how to get an adequate amount to spend, and live in incredible poverty.

The little old lady who lives around the corner has Social Security and not much else, but because of her limited income and limited assets, she is entitled to many other benefits —supplementary Social Security, government-subsidized rent, food stamps, Medicaid, and free household help. Add it all together and she has more money to spend on basic living than I do.

Yet, she lives poor and mean with an unmade bed in her cluttered living room. She wears depressing, cast-off clothes and an ancient wig that somebody gave her. She has no hobbies, no pleasures, no resources within herself, no friends, and nothing to do. She complains about everything, condemns everyone, and hoards and hides her money. She does not know how to use the money she has to bring herself happiness or pleasure, and she is so negative and so self-centered that she cannot break out of the shell she has built around herself to live happily and freely. It isn't money she lacks. It's know-how.

I know another old woman who has been on welfare most of her life and lives in an appalling room in a rattletrap hotel. Unkempt and dirty, she looks like a refugee from the ragbag. Seeing her, one yearns to do something to lift her out of the abyss she has created for herself. Is she poor because welfare is inadequate? No, because she spends her money on drugs and drinking.

If you use your head and develop your skills and resources,

it is possible to manage nicely on welfare. But, in order to
have a decent life, you must know how to obtain the benefits to which you are entitled and where to go to apply for
them, and then wait rather patiently until you get them.

People who are in need should inform themselves of the
help that is available. Many times, this is the stumbling block.
They don't know where to get help; they don't even know
about the help that is available; and if they don't apply for
it, they never get it. No one comes around offering it on a
platter. The Social Security office is a good place to start,
then the county welfare office. Don't telephone; go in person
if possible. It's much easier to do business face to face than
over the phone.

The American Association of Retired Persons, an organization for older people, also has access to information about
help for oldsters who need it. In many communities it has an
office where you can talk with "helping persons," people who
know what resources are available and where to go to get
them. These volunteers serve as paralegal aides, and they are
equipped to give you a public benefit checkup to make sure
you are receiving all the benefits to which you are entitled.
They get answers to questions about specific public benefit
programs and can help you deal with the agencies that run
them.

If your income is so low that you can't live decently, you
are entitled to aid. The programs have been set up for people
who need them. Therefore, if you need help, go to the nearest
Social Security and welfare offices, taking your birth certificate, your receipts, and the necessary records and papers with
you. If you can't fill out the forms, get help from someone
who can.

Under no circumstances should you withhold information
or lie the least bit in order to get aid to which you are not
legally entitled. Eventually you will be caught and the aid
taken away. You will be prosecuted if your misrepresentation
was flagrant and willful.

When you do receive the aid to which you are entitled, in most states you will have almost as much coming in every month as the rest of us who are not eligible for these benefits because we do have some emergency money in our savings accounts. If you have a little but not very much—not really enough to do you any good but enough to keep you from receiving extra benefits—it might be well to spend enough of it so that you could receive benefits such as food stamps, Supplementary Social Security, Medicaid, and household help. You could get a paid-up burial policy, a warm coat, a new color television set, a supply of canned goods to stock your cupboard, or some new clothes, or take a trip, or do whatever else would bring you pleasure. Then you would be eligible to apply for benefits such as food stamps, Medicaid, and so on. But, don't give your money or your property to someone else in order to reduce your assets. This is dishonest and unintelligent. It is never intelligent to give your money or your property away in large amounts.

We all know elderly people who gave all or most of their money and their property away to relatives, expecting to be loved and cared for in their last years, and wound up neglected and miserable as well as penniless. Keeping your money and your property in your own name tends to make relatives a bit more solicitous. Remember that when you are tempted or are being conned into making a generous gesture that you may well live to regret.

3.

Making and Living on a Budget

When you know how much you have coming in every month, the next step is to make a budget. Decide how much you'll spend for basic living and how much you'll save (if any) for emergencies and for little extra treats such as trips, an occasional luxury, or a generous gesture now and then.

I can now live on $130 a month. This takes care of my food, household needs, fun, transportation, gifts, dental and health care, insurance, newspaper, and phone—everything but rent and utilities (which are included in my rent). This is after I got myself together, of course—after I had my apartment furnished to my liking (very cheaply) and got my clothes in shape (very cheaply) and plugged all the loopholes in my spending (quite a few). I live very nicely on this amount. I have everything I need and almost everything I want. I enjoy myself extravagantly. I don't feel at all poor.

Almost everyone I know spends more on living. Most people are amazed when I tell them how little I spend for basic living and how cheaply I can live these days in spite of inflation.

I know some old ladies who live comfortably on even less. They live in small towns in the Midwest or South, usually in their own little houses where they've lived most of their lives, and their needs and wants are very simple.

Before I retired, I spent between $700 and $800 a month on basic living, but I didn't live much better than I do now, and I didn't enjoy life nearly so much. I have become a true do-it-yourselfer. I have learned to make almost everything I need. I perform many services myself that I used to pay for. Time takes the place of money.

Finding Out Where Your Money Goes

Before you can make a budget that suits you, you must know exactly where your money goes. So, you keep track of your expenses for a month or two, you write down every cent you spend and what you spent it for, and at the end of the month you total everything to know how much you spent for food, clothes, doctors, taxis, cleaning, newspapers, and so on. Almost everyone is surprised when she does this, surprised and chagrined at how much she is literally throwing away.

When I did this, I discovered that I had spent fifteen dollars on cigarettes, eight dollars on liquor, twenty-six for films, flashcubes and developing; forty dollars for one pair of shoes; six dollars for books and magazines, eight dollars for a gift for a new baby; twenty-two dollars at the beauty parlor; three dollars on long-distance phone calls; four dollars on cleaning; seven dollars on taxis—all in one month.

I saw immediately where I could cut down on my spending or cut out some of it altogether. (This involved changing my life-style somewhat.) I don't need to smoke and drink; I feel much better when I don't. Had I shopped more carefully, I could have bought shoes for twenty-five dollars—or for sixteen if I had bought at the end of the season when I should have. I don't need to go to the beauty parlor; I can learn to fix my own nails and do my own hair. Clothes that need cleaning are from now on a no-no. I can read the magazines at the library and pick up a couple of books to bring home. Photography is an expensive hobby; I have had to learn to take better and fewer pictures.

The solution to the gift problem is to make a few gifts for new babies, new brides, and birthdays to keep on hand so I always have something to give. A homemade gift, thoughtful and well-done, need cost only two or three dollars. A card, sent two or three days in advance, eliminates the necessity of making long-distance telephone calls; I resolved to write letters instead of calling. Rather than taking taxis, I walk or ride the bus and carry my groceries home in my backpack.

It takes a little practice and a little restraint to go from $750 a month to $130, but it can be done, and now I have money left over from my monthly retirement income to be saved for something I really want, such as a nice, long trip every year or two.

Making a Budget You Can Live With

After you have analyzed your spending, you are ready to make a budget. My monthly budget now looks like this:

Food	$30.00
Insurance	15.00
Paper, phone	10.00
Clothes	10.00
House and gifts	10.00
Fun	10.00
Living money	30.00
Extras	15.00
Total	$130.00

My food budget might seem to be low, but I have schooled myself to eat lightly and healthfully. I also rent a little summer garden and raise my own vegetables, and I barter services with friends in the country for food. When I eat out, I have a dinner salad, nothing else.

I make all my own clothes except for shoes and stockings and underwear. I take good care of my clothes and they last a long time. I buy coats with gift money.

The fifteen insurance dollars are for health insurance, which I never use but dare not be without. I have no life or burial insurance. My body will go to the university medical center. Most of my fun is free. I go to free concerts, lectures, plays, hobby shows, art galleries and museums, and senior citizen activities. Class fees also come out of my fun money.

Things for the house and for gifts are mostly handmade. I already have furniture; one could not buy furniture and household appliances on ten dollars a month. I have no doctor or drug bills as I am never sick or ailing—perhaps because I eat lightly and healthfully and walk almost everywhere I go. I rarely call a taxi; I ride the bus, and I have friends with cars.

I use the "extra" money for such things as permanents and haircuts, getting my teeth cleaned, a supply of vitamins, having film developed, and little trips. There is always a place for this money, and it never goes quite far enough. I may have to nip into my emergency money when a filling unexpectedly falls out of a tooth.

Everything else comes out of my living money—cosmetics, bus fares, stamps, cards, and odds and ends. Thirty dollars a month is a dollar a day. If it costs more than a dollar, don't buy it! It's really amazing how little one needs.

Managing the Budget

Every month, I write a check for my rent, and a check for cash in the amount of $130, all I plan to spend for the month. I keep my food money in a separate coin purse, my living money in another one, and my "extra" money in the teapot. I pay my insurance, phone bill, and the paper boy on the first of the month, and I cache the rest of the money in my budget envelope, a little felt thing with appropriate compartments that I designed and made myself.

If I spend only six dollars for clothes one month, I leave the extra four dollars in the compartment and add ten dollars to it the next month. Occasionally I transfer money from one compartment to another, but not very often.

This is a simple way to live on a budget—one does not need to be a mathematical wizard, or even very bright, to manage a budget like this. One does not charge things with this budget. Poor people cannot afford to pay the carrying charges; the not-so-poor can't afford it either, but many times they don't realize it. The only kind of charge account *we* should have is the kind you pay off in thirty days without any carrying charges at all. If you don't have quite enough in the appropriate compartment to pay for something you need, you charge it.

When the bill arrives thirty to fifty days later, you'll have added another month's allotment to your compartment and can pay the bill in entirety. It's better to stay on a strictly cash basis if possible. If you don't have enough money in your emergency savings account to cover an occasional slip-up, you should turn in your charge cards and remove yourself from temptation.

Things to Consider When Making Your Budget

Where you live makes a big differences in how much you must spend to live nicely. Remember this when you make your budget. I came to the Middle West from the San Francisco Bay area. Living in the Bay area now would cost me two or three times as much as it does here. Food is higher there; services are higher; getting around is higher; rent is out of sight. Of course, this is something to consider when you decide where you will live when you retire.

Your lifestyle will make a difference. Your personal preferences will make a difference. When you make a budget, you will make choices expressing your preferences. Would you rather have steak or another pair of shoes? Would you rather call your children long distance or give them a present? We all have to make choices. The important thing is to make the right ones for you.

You may want to consider changing your lifestyle. I changed mine and found a new and happier way of living. Since retirement, my tastes have become very simple, and I have lost all desire to possess. I still like to look at beautiful, expensive things and admire them, but I have no wish at all to own them.

At a party recently I heard someone ask a charming, middle-aged man how he was able to retire at forty-three. He replied, "I have a wife who doesn't want anything."

Neither do I, because I have the things I value most— leisure to do exactly as I wish, time to use exactly as I please. I am, at last, completely free to decide what I will do with these gifts. These are the magic keys to a happy, fulfilling, and rewarding old age—leisure and time, and the privilege of deciding how they will be used. What more does anyone need?

4.

Deciding Where You Will Live

Where you live will determine to a large extent how much you need to live nicely. A big city is usually more expensive than a smaller city. A tiny town or hamlet is usually the cheapest of all. This may not be true if the tiny place is in a resort or in what is considered a desirable area. The more desirable the area, the more expensive it will be. Living in the Midwest or the South is usually cheaper than living on the East or West Coast.

Many older people simply decide to stay right where they are and manage however they can. In many cases, this is the best solution, especially if you have friends and family where you are. Moving away from the familiar and starting a new life in a new place is difficult for some older people, especially if they do not make new friends easily or if they have difficulty adapting to change.

Of course, some people are so sufficient within themselves that they do not need many friends or other caring people around them. They like being alone and are never lonely.

This type of person would probably be able to adapt anywhere —as would the person who does make new friends easily, enjoys change and variety, and welcomes new experiences and opportunities.

Do you want to make a move? Or, are you happy where you are? Only the individual herself can and should decide this, and you should not let other people influence your decision unduly.

I know a woman with adequate income and a house worth $60,000 who struggles along attempting to care for her house and garden herself, not enjoying it at all. She would really like to sell the house and move into a cozy little apartment on the beach and travel a bit, but she doesn't because her only son discourages this. He wants the house, so she is "saving" it for him instead of taking her life in her own hands and living it the way she would like.

Before you make a major move of any kind, you should try out the locale and the arrangement for six months or so, keeping yourself in a very fluid state while doing it, so you can escape to something else if it is not entirely to your liking. Before I returned to the Middle West from California, I spent a delightful summer here. That wasn't long enough. I should have managed to spend a winter here before deciding. I had forgotten how long and grey and dreary a Kansas winter can be.

However, if an unfortunate decision or move has been made, one does *not* need to be stuck with it permanently. You can make plans to get out of it. I am making long-range plans to return to California eventually, and in the meantime I enjoy myself thoroughly in the spring, summer, and fall and take my yearly trip in the dead of winter.

There are many ways of getting around an unfortunate situation besides putting up with it or adapting to it. If you find yourself in any situation not to your liking, the thing to do is to start making plans to get out of it. There is always a way, and if you start thinking constructively and creatively about it, you will think of something; you will find a way to do whatever you really want to do if you have the necessary courage and stamina.

Most older women are sufficiently intelligent not to move in with their family permanently, even though this may be the cheapest possible choice. Moving in is almost always a disaster for the family or for the woman herself and usually for both. It disrupts a family to have an older person thrust suddenly and permanently upon it, even though the family may be patient and loving, and it is certainly not good for grandmother or auntie to give up her autonomy and endure the confusion and commotion of the younger generation for twenty-four hours a day or to be expected to serve as an unpaid babysitter and houseworker, which happens all too often. There are other and better ways of coping with the problem of where you will live and how you will manage.

Sudden widowhood can cause a woman to do foolish things, however. Numbed with grief and shock, she is unable to think or to plan intelligently and makes unwise decisions that she will regret later. Probably the best thing to do is to stay where you are until you are able to think clearly again and to plan.

One *should* have thought this through and made plans beforehand, of course. The possibility of being suddenly widowed and suddenly alone is always near when one is older. Everyone should consider this before it happens: What will you do? Where will you go when you find yourself suddenly alone? Many times the shock is lessened and the grief not so intense when one is prepared for action. Widowhood may in fact be a release for some women, free for the first time in years to do exactly as they please. Once they get used to it, they may enjoy being alone.

Though few older women will willingly make the mistake of moving in with their families, there are a good many who will make cross-country moves to be closer to their children; this can also sometimes be a mistake. I know a lady named Elaine who gave up her house and her job in the Middle West to take an apartment in San Antonio, where her married daughter had lived for twenty years. She had been there but six months when her daughter's husband was transferred to the East Coast. Her first move was quite expensive, and Elaine cannot afford to move again so soon. Now she is alone in San Antonio, much more alone than she would have been in the Midwest, where she had many friends.

There are other things to be considered before deciding to move close to one's children. It is a rare granny and a remarkable mother-in-law who can remain discreetly silent when she sees those near and dear to her making what seem to her to be mistakes in judgment and fouling up their lives. It takes great self-control not to give them the benefit of your experience and tell them what they should do. Even though your advice is well-intentioned and may be sound, the younger generation will resent your well-meant advice—and rightly so!

Since they are adults, they must be allowed to make their own decisions, choices, and mistakes, and to find their way out of dilemmas without advice or assistance—or even too much concern—on the .part of mother or grandmother or aunt. Even unspoken disapproval can lead to unpleasant complications and confrontations. One can often be much happier not knowing about the problems adult children face.

Neither should you move close to your family because you think they will do things for you, or because you expect them to look after you. You stand a good chance of being very hurt if they don't; you may become very disillusioned when they are too busy or too involved with other things to give you the attention you feel you deserve.

Waiting on an able-bodied parent and doing distasteful little chores such as putting up her pictures, washing down her walls, or taking her to the grocery are responsibilities adult children should not be expected to assume if you give little or nothing in return. Such help is an imposition and is not good for you either. It fosters dependence when you should become independent. It turns you into a helpless, demanding old woman when you should be growing in the ability to stand alone, polishing up your old skills and learning new ones, and developing self-reliance and self-awareness. It is simply unrealistic to expect adult children to look after you, wait on you, and take care of you. Moving close for these purely selfish reasons leads to helplessness and unhappiness.

Too close an association with family sometimes impedes the growth of an older person. Families know you as you are and as you have been, not as you are going to become. When someone close to you thinks of you in a certain way, you tend to think that way of yourself. When we were discussing this recently, a friend told me: "I feel much freer and more of a person when I am not around my family. I feel free to become, to grow, and to change as I wish. I feel held back, inhibited, hemmed in, and bound by family. They know me as I was, not as I am, not as I am becoming."

If they gave themselves a chance, many older people might find it easier to share of themselves with others than with family who have preconceived and set ideas of them and their roles. Some women *prefer* to adore their families from a distance; one very realistic mother maintains that mothers-in-law, like children of yesteryear, should be seen and not heard —and not seen too often either. She says visits should be short and sweet—and if short enough, they probably will be.

If the image of the granny who lives only for her family or the fond auntie who just can't do enough for everybody suits you, you will be happiest living in the midst of family. If you have a warm, close, loving relationship with your family, you may want to move as close to them as possible—though not in with them. If you can develop a live-and-let-live attitude, you will feel comfortable, safe, and secure being close.

But, if you don't have this kind of relationship with your family, or even if you do but can't afford to live near them, or if you simply prefer to create a completely independent and satisfying life of your own, you can develop this kind of relationship with other people—but you may have to work at it a bit harder. There will always be people who need you and will want to know you—a warm, understanding older person, interested and interesting. Be that kind of person and you will never need to worry about being alone unless you want to be.

Whatever you decide to do—stay where you are, move to a less expensive area, or move close to your family—once there, do start immediately to get out and around and create a life of your own apart from your family. Expand your horizons.

Do it first physically—on foot, if possible. Get out and explore the neighborhood, poke around in the stores and shops, and find out where everything is. Get on a bus, any bus, and ride to the end of the line. This is a marvelous and inexpensive way to explore a new city. Senior citizens can usually ride for half fare, and for a few dollars you will have seen everything and learned where everything is.

Get a map of the city so you'll know where you're going and where you've been. Get the brochures from the chamber of commerce, and read the guides that tell the tourists what to do. Locate the library, the parks, the churches, the art galleries, the museums—all the interesting places where tourists go and the natives have never been.

If you are a joiner, join the woman's club; if you are a churchgoer, go to church; if you like games, join a senior citizens' group. Whatever you like to do, do it—alone at first, if need be. You'll soon meet someone to do it with you. In a couple of months you'll know the new area like the back of your hand, and you will find it much more fascinating than if you had sat at home and eyed it from a distance.

Even if you don't go anywhere new, now that you have the leisure and the inclination, discover or rediscover your own city or town this way. Don't stay in your rut if you're in one, though it may be safe and comfortable. Get out of it and explore the possibilities around you.

5.

Finding the Right Place to Live

When you have decided where you will live, what will you live in—a house of your own, a condominium, a mobile home, a rented apartment, a retirement home, a hotel room, or a shared accommodation of some kind?

The more money you have, the more options you have, and the more choosey you can be about your living arrangements. When you have very little money or don't want to spend all you have on a place to live, your choices are definitely limited. But that doesn't mean you can't live nicely if you choose carefully and are willing to spend some time and effort fixing up a place to your liking. A little money goes a long way when you do the work yourself.

A Place of Your Own

Buying a house, a condominium, or even a mobile home—unless it's secondhand—is probably too expensive. Unless you are already somewhat decrepit, you can live much more cheaply and rather more gaily outside a retirement home.

There are two kinds of retirement homes, the posh kind for old ladies with money, and the plain kind for poorer old ladies who can barely get around. To get into either kind, you must usually make an initial down payment ranging from moderate to large, depending on how luxurious the accommodations are.

Most of us will dismiss the idea of buying a place to live. However, if you already have a house you don't want to sell and it's costing you a fortune to keep up, you might consider taking in a roomer or two. Roomers can be a headache. But, they need not be if you select them carefully, lay down the ground rules before they move in, and can be hard-boiled about evicting those who won't play by your rules or who don't pay their rent promptly. If you don't know your roomer, it's best to exchange references. If everything is in writing, signed and legal, you should have little trouble getting rid of them if they prove unsatisfactory; do this even if it's someone you've known for years.

You can't always take in roomers, of course, even though you may want to. There may be zoning regulations prohibiting it, or you may not find anyone suitable who wants to room with you. Check with the proper authorities first; don't spend a lot of money getting set up to become a landlady until you feel out the situation.

Disadvantages of Living Alone in a House

Living alone in a house is simply not safe these days, in my opinion. Every day, one reads in the paper that some woman living alone has been attacked or beaten up or even murdered in her bed. This happens to "nice" women too, not only to those who frequent bars unescorted late at night and associate with scruffy companions. Attacks can and do happen in places other than a house, of course, but living alone in a house seems to me to be inviting trouble. The only house I would venture to live in alone would be in a tiny, conservative town with a low crime rate, close to congenial neighbors, and with a small dog with a big bark.

When you live in your own house, there are certain responsibilities you must accept. These involve the maintenance of the heating system, the plumbing, the grounds, and the exterior of the house. Furnaces must be fixed, sidewalks repaired, screens taken down and put up, the house painted, the lawn mowed, flower beds weeded, and hedges trimmed. In fact, most of your time in good weather will be devoted to exterior maintenance. Inside, there are leaky faucets, stopped-up plumbing, tiles that come unstuck, and carpets that need cleaning. If you have to hire these things done, it will cost you a fortune—if you can find someone to do it. With taxes, upkeep, and maintenance both inside and out, a house for a woman alone is usually no bargain. If you don't keep up the house and grounds, they deteriorate rapidly in both value and appearance, and you'll soon feel that you're living in a slum —and everyone else, including prospective buyers, will think so too.

It's easier to live in a little apartment. If something goes wrong, all you do is contact the management, and (with luck) whatever is wrong will be repaired, replaced, or otherwise taken care of. It doesn't always work that way, of course. Sometimes management is lax, and the plumbing can be stopped up and the garbage cans overflowing in the alley, but you can always report them to the board of health without any compunction at all and force some action of the part of management.

Sharing

Sharing a house is also safer, easier, and more economical than living in it alone. I know several people who share a house compatibly and thus cut down their expenses. A pair of them are sisters. They can live very cheaply together in the house they already own, so they can afford to hire most of the outside work done.

Another pair are friends. Each does her own cooking and her own grocery shopping; each has her own shelves in cupboards and refrigerator. They make a point of going out alone

—each has her own friends and activities—and they divide the cleaning tasks, housekeeping chores, and yard work. They share only the house and the rent, not their lives, and each finds it satisfactory, as they are able to live quite cheaply and more safely together.

An example of an unsual and ideal sharing situation is four friends who together rent a big, old-fashioned house owned by the son of one of them. Each has her own bedroom, and each has a talent or skill that she contributes to the group. They look after each other, help each other in all kinds of ways, and contribute to a kitty for expenses. By sharing, they are able to survive and enjoy life much more together than separately.

People who share have to be pleasant, easy-to-get-along-with people who are tolerant and flexible and who can adapt and adjust to change and another's ideas, feelings, and moods. There should be some provision for complete privacy—a room of one's own or someplace where one can get away from everybody else and just enjoy being alone.

A Mobile Home

A trailer or mobile home is great if you have a husband or a car, or preferably both. But, since you are alone and poor and don't have either, there are drawbacks as well as advantages. Mobile homes are compact and cozy. There's a world of storage space and so many built-ins that little furniture is necessary. But, living alone in a trailer or mobile home parked in an ordinary trailer park isn't safe either. You are probably miles away from everything, and often there is no public transportation close enough to do you any good. If you do find a pleasant place to park your home, the rent is no doubt sky-high; if it isn't sky-high, the trailer park is probably very crowded and rather slummy. Even when anchored properly, trailers and mobile homes are usually the first things blown away or otherwise destroyed when a tornado descends or a hurricane hits, and some of the smaller ones rock and sway uncomfortably on a windy day.

Sometimes a trailer or small mobile home can be parked in the backyard of a family member or friend, and you can take cover in his or her basement in case of storms and feel perfectly safe at other times. But, be sure to check everything out with the proper authorities before you go out and buy anything; you can run into zoning problems and other complications.

Hotel Living

If you hate housekeeping and like eating out, and if you don't want to be bothered with a lot of personal possessions or don't have any and don't want to acquire any, hotel living may be for you. There are hotels made to order for retired people. Some of these older hotels were at one time *the* hotel in the city's center, but when stores and businesses moved to the shopping centers on the outer edges of the city, the hotel was left there with nobody in it; therefore, the rooms are rented at a reasonable monthly rate to retired and elderly people.

I have a friend who lives in one of these hotels in a resort area in California, and she finds it the perfect solution. She is a person who likes to read, watch television, play bridge, visit, work crossword puzzles, eat out, and travel. Living in a hotel enables her to do everything she likes and to avoid everything she doesn't—such as cooking, shopping, keeping house, entertaining, and getting involved with a lot of personal possessions.

At the hotel there is daily maid service, two meals a day to be had in the dining room at a price she can afford, a cozy lobby, an atmosphere of quiet and genteel refinement, public transportation at her door, and a delightful mall only a stone's throw away.

The hotel appears to be safe and respectable—it has an air

of rather seedy elegance which is quite charming. There are hotel rooms to be had for very little rent, but these are usually a bit more run down or not in a desirable area, and they should be carefully evaluated before you move in.

When living in a hotel it is possible to save considerably by eating part of the time in the room. One little lady told me she keeps a box of cereal and some fruit and skim milk powder in one corner of the bureau drawer, and she breakfasts in her room on cereal and fruit and tea. She dresses up and goes out every day for lunch—not to a restaurant or the hotel dining room, but to a government-subsidized lunch program for the elderly—and again eats in her room at night.

A Rented Apartment, Furnished or Unfurnished

Many women living alone will be happiest in a rented apartment, either furnished or unfurnished, but finding a comfortable, attractive, safe place that you can pay for is not the easiest thing to do these days. Even if you have unlimited funds, it's not always easy to find one exactly to your liking. How much you can afford to pay will depend on your total monthly income. Ideally, you should not pay more than a quarter of your income, but you may have to go somewhat higher than that and economize more stringently on other things in order to find a safe place in an area where you want to live. You can start by calling the apartments listed in the yellow pages of the telephone book, but these will usually be the more expensive apartments. What you are looking for is a nice apartment for practically nothing.

You can find one if you leave no stone unturned. Try everything—even apartment locaters and brokers who will charge you a fee to put you next to current and expected vacancies. Sometimes these people can save you untold time and frustration—and money, in the long run. You can tell them exactly what you're looking for, the price you can pay, and the area or areas you want to be in. If they don't have anything or can't find anything for you, you need not pay. (Don't go to the kind you must pay whether they find you anything or not.) These people can be of real help if you're new in an area and need an apartment at once.

But often, with a little bit of luck, you can find a place yourself without any fee at all by beginning your search in the classified rental listing of the local papers. There will usually be more listings in the Sunday papers, but don't ever wait until Sunday to start calling and looking. Get an early edition of the Sunday paper on Friday evening or early Saturday morning and start immediately. Other people do this, too, and as a result the more desirable places are often rented before noon on Saturday. Everything good will have been snapped up before Sunday when the uninitiated start looking.

Many desirable apartments are rented without ever being advertised at all. To find one of these, you must be more than a little lucky and not at all bashful. Let all your friends and acquaintances know that you are looking and what you would like. Having a wide circle of friends helps. The more people you have helping you, the greater the chance of finding something good. Part of the luck is knowing a lot of people.

A friend of mine found an ideal apartment this way. A couple had created an attic apartment in their home for an elderly relative which had been vacant since her death. Someone told my friend, and she called and persuaded them that she would be an ideal tenant, a fact verified by the person who had told her about it.

Some people put their own advertisements in the paper under the heading of "Apartments Wanted." This is especially good if you are willing to work part-time for all or part of the rent. A friend of mine found an apartment this way— she answers the phone two evenings a week and on Sunday. This necessitates her being there at these times and interferes with her social life somewhat, but she has a beautiful apartment at a price she can afford to pay.

If you are the kind of person who talks easily to strangers, you can pump everyone you meet to see if they know of available apartments—store clerks, people you meet casually while waiting for the bus, and people who sit beside you at the lunch counter. I have found apartments this way. I also found apartments in San Francisco by simply going up and down the streets in an area where I wanted to live and looking at mailboxes. If there were boxes with no names, I rang the manager to inquire if there were vacancies.

When looking for an inexpensive apartment, you can't be excessively choosey. Don't expect to find an apartment in a fashionable neighborhood, but don't settle for one in a slum either. You aren't going to take just any old thing (for any length of time, that is) to get in off the street. The neighborhood should be reasonably respectable and the building safe with locks and chains on the doors and bars or grids on first-floor windows. There should be fire extinguishers in evidence, and fire exits and escapes should be well marked. The building should appear to be reasonably well maintained, although the halls and lobbies of many apartments are not spotless and gleaming these days. But, it doesn't matter if these things are a bit seedy as long as you can make your living quarters attractive. Does the place have possibilities? A can or two of paint, a new piece of carpeting, and some imagination and ingenuity will work wonders. You can often save money in the long run by renting a run-down place and fixing it up.

Apartments for the Elderly

Since we are old and poor, we do have some advantages over younger working people when it comes to finding an apartment. In almost every city and town of any size, there are apartment complexes built specifically for elderly and handicapped people with low incomes.

These apartments are not spacious or posh, but they are adequate and can be fixed into charming, attractive little nests for one or two. Some of these are subsidized to a certain extent by the federal government, and the rent varies, depending on income. Usually you will pay about one-quarter of your income for rent and utilities.

Sometimes, church groups build and manage apartment complexes for the elderly. In many cases, these too are less expensive than comparable apartments in the city. One does not need to be a member of the church to live in a church-sponsored complex.

When looking for an apartment, it would certainly be well to investigate these places. You can get a list of the ones available from the local chamber of commerce. Visit the complexes and inspect the halls, the lobby, and the laundry room. Talk with the manager, and look at the various apartments if there are vacancies at the time of your visit. There usually won't be, as these apartments are a good deal for older people, and there is usually a waiting list so that when an apartment is vacated, someone moves in immediately. The manager may, with the tenants' permission, let you look at apartments that are occupied, however. You may also get to meet some of the present tenants that way.

The apartments may seem to be very small, especially if you have been used to living in a larger, more spacious place, and you will find all kinds of people living in these buildings. For example, you may find a little lady, a retired woman-of-all-work, who has a Social Security income of $160 a month. Because her income is low, she is eligible for many other benefits and manages nicely in her little $40-a-month apartment. Down the hall from her may be the widow of the dean of the law school of a prestigious university, a completely charming and cultured woman who pays the maximum rent. Across the way may be a former buyer for an exclusive dress shop, still chic and sharp in her seventies, who pays somewhere in between. There may be retired nurses and teachers and office workers, and a few couples fortunate enough to be living out their last years together—all of them paying various amounts of rent, depending on their incomes.

There are disadvantages to living in these places. They *are* small, and you live in the very midst of only older and handicapped people, many of whom are feeble and ailing and approaching senility. At times this can be rather depressing. However, in my opinion, the advantages outweigh the disadvantages. First, they are cheap—cheaper than anything comparable in the city. They are usually well located and convenient to shopping and public transportation. They have laundry rooms and recreation rooms and locks and chains on the doors. Some of them have such facilities as exercise rooms and saunas. Some have basement lunchrooms where subsidized meals are served every noon. This enables one to live very cheaply and provides a bit of socialization for those who don't get around much.

In some areas, a bus will take the tenants on a two-hour shopping trip to a different shopping center every week. A nurse comes in one afternoon a week and will check blood pressure, listen to complaints, advise, and console. People who like games can get together in the recreation room for cards in the evening. Most of these apartments have lobbies for sitting and visiting, and the doors are locked after five o'clock in the evening and unlocked in the morning when the manager comes on duty, so they are reasonably safe. There are usually call systems in each apartment and someone on duty to take calls when sudden illness or some other emergency strikes the older person without warning.

It is possible to live very cheaply and very comfortably in these places. They are usually painted and thoroughly cleaned before you move in, so you will not have to spend days scouring someone else's mess off the stove or removing their stains from the rug. That's already been done.

When you find the right place for you, you will have to make application and be accepted and then be put on a waiting list and wait for a time to move in. If you appear to the manager to be a desirable tenant, he or she may slip you ahead of others on the waiting list who do not appear to be so desirable. An experienced manager can usually spot a desirable tenant by talking with her. A desirable tenant appears competent and organized. She is one who will mind her own business, not gossip or quarrel with other tenants, and follow the rules in regard to trash disposal and use of the laundry rooms. She pays the rent on time, keeps noises to a minimum, does not bother management with complaints about trivia, and will not expect preferential treatment or special services.

It pays to be a desirable tenant. Being rude or ugly seldom improves a situation and may do harm. A friend of mine once told a manager exactly what she thought of him—her opinion of him was not high—and was chagrined several years later to find him managing an apartment complex she very much wanted into. Naturally, she didn't get in.

Before dismissing these "older people" places, remember that many managers do not want to rent to older people. I have been told this frankly. They find that many older tenants are fussy, helpless, and prone to illness and require looking after. But, the places built specifically for older and retired people welcome us and wait for us. In fact, they can't be rented to anyone else.

I feel very fortunate that I was able to move into one of these places. My little three-room apartment is comfortable, cozy, and shining clean, with individually controlled heating and air conditioning, carpeting, an electric kitchen, a garbage disposal, and a modern bathroom with a tub and shower that work at the flick of a finger. The building is on a downtown corner, close to public transportation that takes me anywhere in the city I wish to go. I feel secure and safe at night locked away from the outside world of mugging and street fights. For this I pay only one-quarter of my total income, leaving the rest for eating, playing, living, and traveling.

The right kind of place to live is important, especially when one is older. Most of us spend quite a bit of time at home, and the older we get, the more time we will spend there. It's good for the morale to have a pleasant, comfortable, attractive place to live.

It's interesting and enjoyable to get out and look and keep looking until you find that just-right place. No one ever found the right place by sitting on her hands and engaging in wishful thinking. You have to get out and around and use your initiative and your feet while you still can. Eventually you'll come across a just-right place that you can pay for, and then you can start fixing it up to suit yourself.

6.

Fixing and Furnishing

Attractive living quarters are essential to happiness. If you put it together yourself, it takes only a little money.

Fixing and furnishing take thought, time, and effort. However, the time spent in making and fixing can be some of your happiest hours and when you are finished and stand back to admire—knowing you did it yourself with paint brush, sewing machine, a hammer and pliers, a few scraps, and some glue—it gives you a nice feeling of satisfaction and achievement.

Upon retirement or late widowhood, most of us will seek to create a comfortable, attractive little nest to settle into. The older we get, the more time we'll spend in it, and a dreary, ugly place will grow increasingly depressing with time. Cleanliness, color, brightness, and neatness lift the spirits and make an old heart sing. So, the money and time spent on fixing and furnishing will continue to pay off for years in happiness and satisfaction.

Drawbacks of a Small Apartment

Most of us who move into the small apartments that we can afford on our minimal incomes will be immediately confronted by one or more obstacles—the color scheme being that of the builder, not ours; inadequate or inconvenient storage space; cast-off furniture; a bed in the living room; or a kitchen sink or cabinets projecting into the living room without divider or separation so that we and our company are constantly confronted with the dishes in the sink. Usually the carpeting, if any, has been chosen to withstand wear and staining rather than for beauty.

Do not despair, however. There are ways around all these problems. Be thankful that the place is painted and clean and carpeted. This will save you the work and expense of doing it yourself. If you decide to redo it—and you can if you are reasonably agile—you can choose your own color scheme, but frankly, it's hardly worth it. It is much easier to simply make up your mind to live with the color scheme of the builder, especially if the drapes and carpeting go with the place. Most builders choose rather neutral colors, shades of white or beige or grey that go with almost anything.

What to Do About the Color Scheme

When you move into an aparement and you must take into consideration what is already there—the carpeting, the drapes, and the walls—you take your decorating from there and choose your colors accordingly. If your place is small, the color scheme should be the same throughout.

An old friend of mine created a blue kitchen, an orange and brown living room, a pink bathroom, and a bedroom in lavender and yellow. Each room when viewed alone looks lovely, but when you walk through, the effect is chaotic and jarring. Color is doubly important in a small, cheap place. You want your apartment to look coordinated throughout, even if you have to discard a few things you already have and get something new.

My place had white walls, dark woodwork, gold kitchen appliances and bathroom walls, beige curtains, and beige carpeting speckled busily with gold and brown. The kindest thing that could be said about it was that it wouldn't show the dust. When I did the apartment in gold and brown and yellow and orange which blended with the carpeting and drapes, the carpeting looked much less busy, and the rooms are gay and bright and colorful.

What to Do About Someone Else's Furniture

If you rent a furnished apartment, you will be stuck with the furniture already there, most of which may be pretty bad. Again, do not despair. Soiled and faded upholstered furniture can be covered with slip covers or throws, either purchased or homemade; furniture can be repaired and then painted or antiqued to make it look quite respectable. Dirty carpeting and hopelessly damaged floors can be covered with new carpeting cut by you and laid in place right over the old. If you should move, you can roll it up and take it with you.

A Bed in the Living Room

If you can't throw out the bed in the living room and get a couch or bed divan or some other arrangement that looks like a piece of living room furniture in the daytime, push the bed up against the wall, get a bolster, cover it, make a matching spread, and pile the bed with big, fat, luxurious pillows that you can make yourself by stuffing them with polyester fill. If you buy those big, fat, luxurious pillows, they will cost almost as much as a bed divan, but pillows are easy to make. A narrow single bed decked out with a bolster and pillows can look quite nice in your one-room apartment, and it makes for comfortable lounging in the daytime too.

Room Dividers

You can hide the kitchen cabinets and sink with some kind of divider—glass beads hanging down, a folding door, a decorated screen, a colored plastic room divider on poles that extend from floor to ceiling, a screen or bamboo curtain that pulls down from the ceiling, a standing shelf unit, hanging plants, a drape or curtain on a rod attached to the ceiling, or some other arrangement you dream up to separate yourself from the sink. One friend strung bottle caps on colored twine, which cost her practically nothing. Another made an airy macrame hanging.

Making More Storage Space

Before you think about extra storage space, get rid of every single thing you don't need—clothes, books, cooking utensils, odds and ends, dishes, and luggage that has seen better days. Sell the things you don't need, give them to someone who can use them, or call the Good Will. Old ladies tend to keep and collect and try to live with too many things. A friend tells me that every week she cleans a cupboard or closet and makes a point of disposing of one thing, large or small, which she no longer wants or needs, thus keeping her possessions to a minimum and her rooms uncluttered.

How do you create extra storage space? There are many things we can do without any assistance at all. Most of us are not very adept at hammering and sawing and building. Even if we can do the work, we often lack the proper tools, and a small apartment is no place to do woodworking, as it disturbs the other tenants. A hammer for driving nails, a screwdriver, and a pliers are the only tools you will need for most of these old-lady projects. Some of them require only paste and glue and cardboard cartons and paper. You can solve many of your storage problems by judicious and careful shopping.

One way to make extra storage space is to put a second shelf in the yawning upper reaches of your closet. If you can't install a shelf yourself or get someone to do it for you, get some shoe boxes, stack them, and cut some shelf pieces from a huge cardboard carton. Cover the carboard with paper or cloth, make a shelf edging, and put lightweight objects on the cardboard shelf, which rests on the stacked shoe boxes. Use big tin cans covered attractively instead of boxes if you wish.

Get two or three under-the-bed cardboard storage boxes in which to store out-of-season clothes and bedding. Most of them come in a height to just slip under a bed, but measure both the box and your bed to be sure.

Some kitchen cabinets do not extend to the ceiling, and the space above the cabinets is wasted. If you need it for extra storage, buy or make storage boxes to fit the space and cover them with wallpaper, shelf paper, or self-adhesive paper to match the kitchen decor. You can make boxes the exact dimensions you want by cutting cardboard pieces and taping them together with the very strong tape that movers use to seal their cartons. You can get this tape at an office supply store. Make a lid to fit over the box and cover both with the paper. This is quite a job, but it looks much nicer than if you use boxes of assorted sizes and shapes and coverings. Matching lidded baskets look very nice also, but they are unfortunately rather expensive.

Get a small inexpensive plastic cupboard at the dime store and attach it to the bathroom wall. Put towels in it, and set bath supplies on top.

Get clear plastic storage boxes from the dime store, cover them with paper or material that matches your bedroom decor, and stack them to the ceiling on the closet shelf.

Instead of having end tables, use small chests in which you can store things. Instead of a coffee table in front of the divan or couch, use a wicker or rattan chest or a trunk and store things in it. Get furniture you can sit on and store in, such as a deacon's bench.

Hang long shelves along one entire wall. Store things in attractive baskets and boxes on the shelves.

Put extra shelves under the sink cabinet. Use bricks and a

board which you can have cut for you at the lumber yard. Or get a big lazy Susan and put it under the sink. Put spices and seasonings on a smaller lazy Susan in the cupboard.

Screw cup hooks beneath the shelves of the dish cupboard to hang cups. Screw cup hooks on the inside of cabinet doors to hang brushes and dish mops and other things.

If your cooking utensils are attractive, hang them on a rack above the stove. Store spoons and small kitchen tools in a basket.

Get a zippered shelf arrangement that hangs on a closet pole. Put handkerchiefs, scarves, underwear, and little odds and ends on its cardboard shelves. These closet shelf hangers are expensive, but you can make your own for next to nothing.

Store your shoes and purses in hangers which you can make yourself from sheets and attach to the closet door. If you have folding closet doors, make a floor shoe holder from shoe boxes which you glue together and cover with quilted material. Make a purse hanger which hangs from a closet pole. (Directions for making these things are included in the Mini Make-Do Decorating section in chapter 22.)

Get hangers that hold multiple pairs of slacks and skirts if your closet space is limited. Get clothes poles and shoe racks that hang behind a door. The hardware slips over the door, making for a painless installation. I recently saw a three-shelf bookcase hanging on the back of a door.

By using your ingenuity, it is possible to achieve a neat, uncluttered look even in a small space. A friend who had no place to put her ironing board made a startling cover for it from some wild fabric and hung it on a door for decoration. I didn't have any place to put my stepladder, so I painted it white, decorated it with decals, and used it for a plant stand which shields the stove from view.

Having a place for everything and keeping everything in its place simplifies living, but, do keep a master list of where you put things tacked in each closet. Otherwise, you'll forget and have to spend frustrating hours looking for things. The lists will solve that problem.

Using Your Own Furniture

Many people moving into an apartment won't have to buy furniture; they already have some, and if so, they are in luck. Select the pieces you take with you with care, though. Small, light-weight pieces look best in a small apartment. If you have only big, heavy furniture, consider selling it and buying something more appropriate with the money you get. Rattan or wicker furniture, glass-topped tables, director's chairs, mirrors, and small area rugs are comparatively inexpensive and good in small places.

Crowding a small apartment with wall-to-wall furniture makes it look even smaller than it is. A friend who lives in a tiny, one-room apartment maintains that a couch, a rocking chair, a pair of storage chests, a table, and two chairs are all the furniture one needs in order to live comfortably and entertain easily.

Sparseness and simplicity are attractive, and don't overlook the value of hand-done things to give your apartment warmth and cheer and individuality. A small hooked rug, thick padded hangers in the closet, wall-to-wall carpeting in the bathroom (which you cut and put down yourself), an exquisite needlepoint pillow or chair seat, a beautifully embroidered sampler, a quilted or embroidered wallhanging, and lots of lush houseplants scattered about make a place distinctly yours, and what does it matter that you picked up furniture from someone's attic or garage sale and antiqued it yourself? If you have any flair at all for decorating and plenty of time and patience, you can create a delightful and charming little place for almost nothing.

Where and How to Buy Furniture

Anyone can buy a room full of furniture in one reckless gesture, but, if you want to save money, you shouldn't. You can have a tastefully furnished place without spending a lot of money if you are willing to spend time to comparison shop and search out unconventional places to buy furniture. You buy furniture at auctions, garage sales, thrift stores, second-hand stores, mail order and discount houses, and the dime store—or you may even pick up someone else's discards, right out of the garbage, for free.

If you are somewhat lacking in imagination and talent for decorating—many of us are—or if you question your own taste, a file of ideas clipped from magazines can be of tremendous help in putting your place together. If you haven't saved such clippings, it will pay you to take a week off to go to the library and look through the back issues of magazines such as *Better Homes and Gardens, Sunset,* and some of the other decorating or women's magazines and take notes on things that appeal to you. Many of the projects will be too posh and expensive. Some will require more skill than you presently possess. But, you will get ideas for things that you can do and ways to renovate old and inexpensive furniture to make it look quite elegant.

A friend of mine bought a full-length mirror on sale at the dime store for only $3.98. By gluing some beautiful seashells she had collected to the cheap-looking frame, edging the mirror with rope, and spray painting the whole frame white, she had a very nice mirror, a replica of one she had seen in a magazine.

The inexpensive fiberboard furniture that one finds in discount stores and mail order catalogs can often be covered to make it look like an expensive piece. Who cares what's underneath when a table is covered with an elegant floor-length cloth trimmed with fringe similar to one seen in a magazine?

Another friend bought a sturdy fiberboard chest. Copying from a picture in a magazine, we covered it with a dotted print and decorated it with felt cutouts, and it became a focal point of her room.

The things that people sell at garage sales and even the throwaways they put in the garbage are often perfectly useable; as you become adept at fixing and repairing, you can salvage them satisfactorily.

When I moved into my present apartment, I had very little furniture, and I shopped for tables and storage pieces and extra chairs at garage sales, thrift stores, and secondhand places. The pieces thus acquired cost me from twenty-five cents to twenty-five dollars. The casual observer does not guess where they came from or how little they cost.

I covered the plastic legs and sides of a pair of twenty-five-cent stack tables with gingham, as I had seen done in a magazine. I tiled the scratched and burned recessed top of a little end table with mosaic tile, and I antiqued the legs. I covered the chrome legs of a glass-topped coffee table with wood-grain Contact paper after being told by a sales clerk that it was almost impossible to cover chrome with any kind of paint. A cheap little rocking chair and a folding chair from someone's garbage were transformed with paint, stencils, and fat cushions made from a fifty-cent bag of scraps plus a yard or two of new material.

It does take elbow grease, imagination, and do-it-yourself techniques to fix and furnish a place inexpensively and attractively. However, anyone of any age can learn these techniques from magazines, books, friends, acquaintances, and salesclerks.

Enlist in-laws and teenage grandchildren to help on the time-consuming and bone-breaking tasks that require more knowledge, skill, and strength than you presently possess. Eventually you will be ready and able to help them and others with your newly learned skills.

7.

Getting It All Together

When you are moving from your own house into a smaller place, probably all you have to do is to decide what you will take with you and then dispose of the rest of your things, always a rather wrenching task. Keep what you take with you to a minimum.

Other than furniture, all you really need are two changes of sheets, a half dozen towels and washcloths, some placemats and napkins, a small tablecloth or two, and dishes and cooking utensils to do your simple cooking and entertaining. That's about all you'll have room for in a small apartment, and there's no reason for having a lot of dishes and linens and pots and pans piled on the shelves.

If you've had crystal and sterling and china and beautiful linens, be glad you had them when you enjoyed and needed them. I hope you'll have no qualms about giving them away to someone who wants them, or selling them or storing them (which can be expensive). If you have room, you can take them with you, of course.

When I moved out of a larger and posher apartment for the last time, I disposed of all those items, knowing I would never need them again and preferring to use the money they brought on travel. I find that expensive possessions or too many possessions of any kind are limiting; they limit one's movement, narrow one's life, and get in one's way. It's much more difficult to maneuver when you are burdened with possessions. The problem of what to do with them and where to put them is always with you.

When I moved into my present apartment, I had to start from scratch and assemble and collect the few things I needed to live comfortably and happily. Unless you are a do-it-yourself person (or become one), you will have to settle for less attractive things or spend much more. A do-it-yourselfer can create some beautiful and novel things for almost nothing.

Dishes

I made my own dishes, pots, and bowls from clay, pouring the slip into molds at a senior citizens' recreation center. (If you have to buy the greenware and then pay for the paint and firing, you might as well buy a set of dishes.)

A set of dishes for four can sometimes be picked up at a garage sale for practically nothing. By getting into the habit of going to garage sales, you may find, as I did, that you can make do nicely on what others sell for a song. Or, try the dime store and mail order houses, where you can get a set of melamine for very little. Melamine is not posh, but it is practical and adequate for one's purposes, and it's gay and colorful. I shopped in the dime store and cut-rate places for glasses, stainless steel, and cook things, and I avoided department stores and furniture store housewares departments, where these things are expensive.

Appliances

What appliances do you really need? I settled for a toaster, an iron, a blender, a yogurt maker, and a little hand beater in place of a mixer. I comparison shopped for these appliances, and I got the toaster with Green Stamps and the blender from the savings and loan company where I deposited my nest egg. This was a bonus for depositing with them. It pays to investigate and take advantage of all these freebies.

Cook Things

When shopping for cook things, I tried to find those that would do double duty, and I again shopped in the dime store and at garage sales. The lid of a glass casserole doubles as a pie pan. The same glass lid fits a Dutch oven and a nonstick skillet. A double boiler makes two kettles. A bundt cakepan becomes a salad mold. An ovenware dish also comes to the table as a serving dish. When you cook simply for yourself and a few guests, you'll find that you need very few cooking utensils. If you cook healthfully, you won't need many pie tins, cake pans, or rolling pins and such that others must have.

You can make many of the things you need. Save your tin cans and jars. Paint or paper them, use them for canisters and storage. Tall glass jars become keepers for rice, beans, and macaroni; other jars hold juice and water in the refrigerator.

Towels

Beautiful bath towels, hand towels, and washcloths are very expensive these days. I bought only one beautiful set for show and for company; for my own use, I bought a half dozen bigger hand towels from a mail order house for less than a dollar apiece. I prefer these to the larger, more luxurious bath towels as they are easier to store and launder and require less space. Colored towels do not show soil or tattletale grey, and they last for years. White or light colored towels must be bleached, and they wear out faster.

I bought several yards of Turkish toweling on sale and made my own washcloths and fingertip towels. I hemmed a square for washcloths and then buttonholed around the edges with leftover embroidery floss. I cut the fingertip towels sixteen by nine inches, hemmed the edges, sewed leftover fringe on the ends, and embroidered "yours" and "mine" in chain stitch on them. The four-inch bits that were left were pieced together with gingham strips to make dishrags.

A linen or terry dish towel costs less than a dollar on sale at a cut-rate store. Flour sacks for towels cost about eighty cents apiece, if you can find them. When cut in two and embroidered, they average about fifty cents a towel.

Appliance Covers, Plant Pot Covers, and Pot Holders

All these things can be made from inexpensive calicolike polyester and cotton, machine quilted and sewn. I used a Simplicity pattern for the appliance covers because it was easier, but you could cut your own patterns if you wished. The casserole clutch and a mitt pot holder can easily be cut freehand. These matching accessories make the kitchen look coordinated and nice, but they are expensive when you buy them. You can hide your unattractive clay plant pots with tubular covers secured top and bottom with elastic.

Bedding

You can buy two muslin sheets and two pillowcases at a white sale for about ten dollars. I found a set of almost new, white sheets and pillowcases at a garage sale for two dollars. I made the full-size fitted sheet fit the twin bed by tearing it in half, taking out the excess, and seaming it in the center; I then embroidered the top sheet and cases with a design I stamped on with a transfer pattern. (I find this kind of unfrustrating embroidery excellent therapy when loneliness or boredom threaten.) Full-size unfitted sheets can be cut down to fit a twin bed by tearing off a strip at the side and hemming. Keep the excess for patches and other projects.

When buying linens, watch for sales and shop at mail order houses, discount stores, and the dime store. When you remove the sheets from the bed, wash and dry and put them back on the bed immediately, and you'll need only one set of sheets and can also eliminate the tiresome business of folding and pressing.

Instead of an electric blanket and bedspread, consider an energy-saving down-filled coverlet for which you can make a beautiful quilted cover with an undersheet snapped in place to simplify bed making. In England this is called a Continental quilt, and it is like sleeping under a cloud. I helped make a puffy, pieced top for a friend who had such a coverlet, and it is a beautiful and luxurious-looking comforter that also serves as a spread.

Table Linens

When eating alone, consider using placemats instead of tablecloths. They're easier to launder and you can have a clean one every day. Burlap, in colors or natural, makes very inexpensive and quick placemats, dresser scarves, and table runners. Simply cut the size you want and fringe and machine-stitch along the edges of the fringe to keep it from raveling further.

Gingham placemats can be similarly fringed, as can matching napkins. Unbleached muslin or linenlike fabrics can be fringed or trimmed with lace, braid, applique, or embroidery.

If you have a round table and want the cloth to hang attractively to the floor, consider making one out of a sheet. Edge the bottom with ball fringe or with lace hand-crocheted from string. You can make matching napkins from the remains of the sheet. I copied for a friend an eighty-dollar table arrangement seen in a department store. There was a floor-length cloth on a round table which was then covered with a square cloth; there were also matching napkins, and napkin rings, which we made from papier-mâché. The copy cost us only twelve dollars.

For a small square or rectangular table, you can make an exquisitely embroidered or lace-trimmed linen cloth and matching napkins. A project such as this will take some time, but it is worth the effort. It's good for the morale to create real beauty occasionally, even if it is a bit more expensive.

When I entertain more than three or four people, I must use my desk as a buffet table, and from scraps and unbleached muslin I made an attractive table runner and hot dish mats on which to set the food. I cut four-inch squares from scraps of plain and figured yellow, brown, orange, and green print and then pieced them together to make a runner of the desired length. Then, I edged the patchwork with strips of unbleached muslin and sewed a brown strip along each side edge.

To make the hot-dish mats I sewed more of the four-inch squares together to make the mats the size and shape I needed, then inserted doubled quilt batting between them, bound the edges together with bias strips of brown, and tacked them with embroidery floss in the center of each square.

Keeping It Together

Once you get your place together and have everything you really need, it should last for years, and you'll have very few house expenses. Occasionally, you must replace something in the house that wears out or gets ugly, but the ten dollars budgeted with gift money will usually cover that if you can make it or fix it yourself. But, when a blender goes kaput or you decide you must have a new color TV or a major replacement of any kind, these must come out of the money in your emergency savings account. However, out of the money budgeted for house and gifts, you should have enough for things like paper towels, toilet paper, light bulbs, and cleaning supplies.

Discount houses and cut-rate drug stores often have special sales on these items, and, when they do, you can lay in a supply for about half of what you usually pay. When buying detergent, bleach, and scouring powder, buy the store brand rather than the highly advertised brands. If you check the labels, you'll discover that they contain almost the same ingredients, and you'll find they clean and bleach and scour just as effectively as the more expensive advertised brands. Use small quantities of cleaning products to make them last longer. Measure the detergent into the washer, and, unless you're terribly clean or terribly dirty, wash only every two weeks. Measure a capful or less of dishwashing fluid into the sink, and wash dishes only when you have a sink full.

Don't feel you must have all the cleaning and laundry supplies you see and hear advertised on TV. You don't need them, in spite of what the commercials would have you believe. The old standbys such as household ammonia, bleach, scouring powder, and steel wool pads are really all you need.

Salt and vinegar clean most metals satisfactorily, especially copper; soda works beautifully inside the refrigerator and on the outside too. A wet hand and a dry towel cleans mirrors and windows and glass-topped tables when they are not too dirty. Put some ammonia in the empty spray window cleaning bottle along with a bit of water, and discover that it does the job as well as the most expensive window cleaner.

An old T-shirt makes the best kind of dust rag. Or, put on an old pair of cotton gloves and dust with both hands. An old Turkish towel makes a marvelous cleaning rag and mop. An old toothbrush cleans crevices and cracks in stoves and plumbing fixtures. In a small apartment, one does not need a mop. Getting down on hands and knees to wipe up a floor is excellent exercise; stooping over is even better, and you get the floor edges and corners much cleaner than if you used a mop. I think wax is dangerous when one is older, and I never use it.

However, if a product makes a task much easier, quicker, and more pleasant, I am in favor of using it even if it makes the task more expensive. By using these products, you're saving time for other, more enjoyable activities. I wouldn't be without tub and tile cleaner. You spray it on and wipe it off and tile and porcelain and chrome gleam with the flick of a towel Oven cleaner, which you spray on, let set, and then wipe off, enables one to clean a stove in half an hour instead of half a day. Reach in and wipe it out with a long-handled dishwashing mop, which you can also use to mop the floor if you can't get down on hands and knees.

I like the spray-on furniture wax which gives furniture a beautiful sheen and gives the room a pleasant, lemony smell, as does the lemony air freshener when sprayed in closets and cupboards.

To freshen a carpet, you can spray on cleaner and then vacuum it up within twenty minutes or so. To clean a carpet that is badly soiled or to remove spots from a carpet, it is necessary to scrub the foam in with a wet sponge and let it dry overnight before you vacuum. Read and follow the directions on the rug cleaner can.

Once you have your place together, it should be very easy to keep that way. You won't have to spend a lot of time scrubbing and dusting and polishing. When you have it together, you can settle in and enjoy it fully.

8.

Eating on a Dollar a Day

It's possible to eat well—that is, healthfully—on very little, if you shop carefully and plan your meals carefully, keeping both nutrition and economy in mind.

Many of the most expensive foods are downright unhealthful. The prime cuts of meat marbled with fat are not good for us now that we are older and should cut down on animal fat; neither are the rich pastries and desserts or the junk foods that many people consume in quantity, literally throwing their food dollars away.

When the amount of money to be spent on food is limited, you can not afford to spend money on anything but foods that promote health—such as vegetables, skim milk and low-fat cheese, fish, fowl, lean meat, eggs, liver, fruit, plant proteins, whole grain cereals and flours, and a bit of polyunsaturated fat. These are all foods that are comparatively inexpensive.

By eliminating the expensive, unhealthful foods and substituting the healthful ones; by limiting the amount of food eaten; by simplifying food preparation and cooking and wasting nothing at all, it's possible to cut almost any grocery bill in half.

Shopping and Cooking Tips

Shop in Supermarkets

Avoid the small neighborhood stores and delicatessens, which are almost always more expensive than the big supermarkets. There is a small store close to where I live, but I save a dollar or more every time I walk to the supermarket and buy a sack of groceries that I can comfortably carry.

Buy Store Brands

These are almost always a few cents cheaper than the name brands and almost always just as good.

Investigate No Name Brands

See if there are stores in your area that carry "no name" brands of food, on which you will save from 10 percent to 30 percent. These are good but not fancy foods. For instance, the peas in a can may not be all the same size.

Coupons

Save and use coupons, but use them only if it's something you really need. The store brand product may be cheaper than the product with the coupon. The consumer always pays for the advertising.

Fussiness about Food

Learn not to be fussy. You don't need the whole mushroom—the stems and pieces will do. You don't need fruit beautifully packed in glass jars. On a dollar a day, you cannot buy such things as pickles, olives, jams and jellies, and other pretty things in jars; you must look the other way.

Convenience Foods

Avoid buying convenience foods and prepared foods as much as possible. These are almost always more expensive than the real things you make yourself. Convenience foods are for working women who don't have time to spend in the kitchen and for those who have no inclination to do so. But be on the lookout for some convenience foods that really are cheaper than those you make yourself, such as orange juice, powdered coffee, and some cake mixes, such as angel food.

Frozen Foods

When buying frozen vegetables, buy those without the sauces and seasonings included in the package. Add your own seasonings and sauces. Use only the inexpensive frozen vegetables: chopped spinach, peas, chopped broccoli. Use only the inexpensive canned vegetables: beans, corn, peas, spinach, beets, sauerkraut.

Fluctuating Prices

When a food you habitually use becomes exorbitantly expensive, eliminate it entirely or cut down on it. I started using powdered coffee when coffee went to four dollars a pound, and had only a cup in the morning. (If you put powdered coffee in boiling water and then let it boil up, you can hardly tell it from regular coffee.) I have Postum, tea, or lemon juice in hot water at other times—much cheaper.

Impulse Buying

Avoid impulse buying. Buy what you went to the store for and only that. Don't be taken in by some product that looks good or that you don't really need. Store managers resort to all kinds of tricks to get people to buy expensive things they don't need.

Shop from a List

Keep a running grocery list. When you run out of a necessary staple, put it on your list. Before you go to the store, plan your eating for the next few days, then check your recipes to see that you have the necessary ingredients on your list. If you shop only once a week, plan your meals for a week.

Powdered Milk

Use powdered skim milk; this is a cheap form of protein and the cheapest form of milk. Old people need the calcium in milk. It keeps us from getting hump-backed, it keeps our bones from becoming brittle, and it keeps the teeth we have left from decaying.

Bulk Foods

Never buy things in cans that you can buy in bulk and cook yourself, such as beans. Beans are one of the cheapest forms of protein. I always keep some cooked brown, kidney, or garbanzo beans marinating in the refrigerator to add to salads.

Buy in bulk or in large quantities whenever possible and feasible. I buy skim milk powder in boxes that make twenty quarts and last me for a month. I sometimes find this on sale for about twenty-two cents a quart. When bought in small boxes, it averages more than thirty cents a quart. It's often cheaper to buy things you use a lot of by the case—canned vegetables, soup, grapefruit and tomato juice, tuna, and sardines. My friends and I sometimes buy these things by the case, divide them, and share the reduced cost.

Baking

Bake your own bread and rolls from whole-grain flours. I use only whole wheat, unbleached, rye, and soya flours, which I buy at the health food store. Not only is homemade bread cheaper than most bakery bread, but it is also more healthful than the soft, spongy white stuff—and more filling. A two-slice sandwich made with homemade bread and put together with a homemade filling makes a meal, not a snack.

Sandwiches

An economical sandwich is not of cheese or ham or egg or tuna salad. Try a thinning cucumber sandwich with yogurt, or a thick lettuce sandwich, or a bean sandwich, or an alfalfa sprouts sandwich. When you're feeling strong, try an onion slice sandwich. These are economical sandwiches and are delicious on good, filling homemade bread.

Keep Food on Hand

Always keep groceries in the house. Don't let the cupboard or the refrigerator become so depleted that you'll be tempted to run out to the delicatessen and buy a cheese sandwich and potato salad in a carton—or dash to the corner and have a double-sized hamburger for ninety-eight cents and almost 600 calories of white bun and filling. A poor-to-medium dinner at a greasy-spoon restaurant costs four dollars or more with tip, enough to buy food for four days when you fix it yourself.

Presliced Food

Never buy cheese or any other food already sliced in little plastic packages. It's cheaper in the bulk and you can slice your own in the time it takes to separate the paper from the food. I grate a pound of cheese, measure it in ¼ - and ½ -cup portions, wrap it in little foil packages, and store it in the freezer. It keeps well and thaws in a jiffy.

Bread

Round out a skimpy dinner with hot breads—whole wheat and bran muffins, Irish soda bread, cornbread, or oatmeal bread. Toast what's left. Good whole grain bread is the staff of life when you are trying to save money on food.

Breakfast, Lunch, and Dinner

Have a whole-grain cereal, milk, and fruit breakfast. I eat milled bran, which I get from the health food store for fifty cents a pound, with wheat germ and yogurt and a few unsweetened prunes, or hot cooked wheat cereal with a banana and skim milk powder mixed with water, my imitation cream.

Have soup or salad or a sandwich for lunch. If you have a good breakfast, you don't need a big lunch.

Don't prepare and serve a wide variety of food for dinner. Three or four things are enough—a big salad, meat or meat substitute, a slice of whole grain bread, and a simple milk dessert make an adequate dinner for an older person. Or, have a casserole dish containing protein and vegetables, raw vegetable sticks or a salad, hot bread, and a milk and fruit dessert. Or, sometimes have a big, hearty salad garnished with sardines and eggs, and eaten with hot bread.

Fresh Vegetables

The cheapest fresh vegetables in winter are potatoes, carrots, onions, celery, cabbage. Buy these often.

Keep vegetables crisp and crunchy for a week or more by cleaning and storing them as soon as you get home from the store. Clean and peel carrots and store them in ice water. Crisp the cabbage head in ice water, shred it, and store it covered. Clean the celery and store it in a covered container. If something does go limp and unattractive, chop it up for the soup pot.

Leftovers

Throw nothing away. Wash and save all the leavings of the vegetables, the peelings, the onion tops, the outside leaves of the vegetables, and the hearts. Cut them up and make soup for lunch by adding beans, macaroni, and tomato juice with grated Parmesan cheese on top. Save the juice from canned vegetables and the water in which vegetables are cooked for the soup pot also.

Boil the bones of a chicken. Use the bone broth in gravy, soup, or casserole dishes.

Stale bread can be an asset. Make crumbs and croutons out of it. Make French toast. Make milk toast. Make stuffing. Make bread pudding. Make bread and cheese souffles. There are all kinds of recipes for using bread slices and bread cubes and bread crumbs.

Don't ever throw out little "dabs" of food. Save them in the refrigerator—the few vegetables, the cold, unappetizing-looking bit of meat. Chop or grind them. Make a thick, rich white sauce, add a bit of grated cheese and egg yolks and whites beaten separately and have a meat and vegetable soufflé.

Fruits

The cheapest fresh fruits in winter are apples, oranges, and bananas. Canned lemon juice is cheaper than fresh lemons in most areas. Although not as good as juice freshly squeezed from the lemon, it will do when lemons are expensive. Buy the big cans of grapefruit and tomato juice. The juice is usually cheaper than the fruit.

"Free" Food

Use as many things as possible that cost you nothing. I use wheat that I get for nothing as it comes from the combine; I also use black walnuts that I pick up in the woods, and I hull and crack them myself. I dry them in the oven and pick them out in my spare time. I grow alfalfa sprouts in glass jars under my sink. A dollar's worth of seeds makes enough sprouts for a year, and the sprouts are very high in vitamin C.

If you have a green thumb, try growing your own herbs in the kitchen window. Then you won't have to buy seasonings. These home-grown herbs are much nicer and add a gourmet touch to simple fare.

Try growing other things. A friend of mine has an inside window box of strawberries and a tub of cherry tomatoes growing in her living room. She seldom has to buy tomatoes, and she has a delightful conversation piece.

Meats and Eggs

Learn to stretch your meat. Meat is one of the most expensive things you buy. A daily serving of from 3½ to 4 ounces should suffice if you supplement it with inexpensive plant proteins. Put something with meat to make it seem like more. The inexpensive meats are chicken, liver, and (normally) hamburger.

Tuna is a comparatively inexpensive fish and it stretches well. I make a casserole from a can of tuna, spinach, protein bread crumbs, homemade mayonnaise, and grated cheese. This makes enough for four dinners. I wrap the leftovers in portion-size foil packages and freeze them.

The most inexpensive canned fish on the shelves is canned mackerel. I make a mackerel loaf with canned mackerel, cracker crumbs, parsley, celery, onions, and lemon juice mixed with an egg and baked in the oven. A bit of catsup on the top during the last fifteen minutes of baking makes it more attractive. This loaf will make six meals.

Chicken is always a good meat buy. Sometimes I buy what is known as a family budget pack for about three dollars. By combining it with canned soups, cereals, bread crumbs and cubes, and vegetables and biscuits, I can get twenty one-person meals from this. Sometimes I only buy the necks and backs at twenty-five cents a pound and use them in recipes I have created. When buying a chicken, buy it whole and cut it up yourself. You get more pieces this way too. Don't cook it all at once. Freeze the pieces individually and cook only what you need.

A pound of lean ground chuck or hamburger makes six meals. I put bread crumbs and an egg with it, season it with onion soup mix, and make individual loaves with the centers stuffed with grated carrots, celery, onions, and parsley to make them seem bigger. These are baked and stored in the freezer.

Liver is cheap and very good for you unless you have a chloresterol problem. It's low in calories, high in B vitamins, and costs about eighty cents a pound—which makes four meals.

Eggs are usually a good protein buy. I always buy the cheaper, medium-sized eggs. Make omelets and soufflés for a main dish. A beautiful omelet makes elegant company fare. A perfect soufflé is a work of art.

Bad Habits

Get out of the snacking habit. Eat only at mealtime. Snack food is often very expensive food.

Get out of the habit of stopping at restaurants and fast food places for a bite to eat. When you do eat out for social reasons and are paying for your own meal, order a dinner salad. Let people think you are trying to preserve your figure rather than your pocketbook. You are, of course, preserving both.

Avoid buying ordinary food at the health food store if you can. It's almost always more expensive.

Don't buy packaged prepared cereals in boxes. Buy milled bran and wheat germ from the health food store in bulk and mix them. Toast the wheat germ in your own oven and make your own granola. Don't buy quick-cooking rice and oatmeal. Cook your own whole wheat cereal. Don't buy white rice. Buy brown rice, the browner the better.

Cheaper Substitute Foods

Be on the lookout for inexpensive substitutes for expensive ingredients. Cocoa and chocolate are expensive. A good substitute is carob powder, which you buy at the health food store. It's cheaper and better for you.

Instead of butter, buy margarine made with vegetable oil.

I buy the cheapest kind I can find and whip it to make it go further. Sometimes I add herbs and make herbed butter.

Buy nuts in the shell and crack them yourself. You usually save money by picking them out. Those in the packages are not as fresh and are not good for you if they are even slightly rancid. Spanish peanuts with the skins are the cheapest packaged nuts you can buy. Whip up a bit of homemade peanut butter from these by adding a bit of oil and milling in the blender. Hulled sunflower seeds which you can buy in bulk, take the place of nuts in some recipes and are almost as good. I sprinkle these over salads and casseroles for added crunch.

Make inexpensive imitations of the real thing, substituting for the expensive ingredients. I make an imitation cheese cake that costs less than a dollar and tastes almost like the real thing.

Entertaining

Don't stop entertaining and having people in to eat. You can still have company on a dollar a day if you time your entertainment—the earlier in the day, the cheaper. Invite people for Sunday breakfast. Have a fruit compote and delicious bran muffins. Or, have people in for morning coffee and serve it with fresh bread. (Guests give you an excuse for eating goodies yourself once in a while.)

Have an afternoon tea. Serve tea and a variety of tea biscuits made from raised biscuit dough.

Invite guests to lunch instead of to dinner, and then have only a beautiful salad garnished with some protein, hot fresh bread, and a very light dessert.

Take festive but inexpensive dishes to pot-luck dinners, not something that costs three or four dollars to fix. I take things such as sweet and sour carrots that look and taste lovely but cost less than a dollar.

To establish or maintain a reputation as a good cook, dream up a few goodies that are absolutely delicious but inexpensive. A friend of mine makes a prune whip pie, which is not at all expensive as it is made from egg whites, sugar, and a few prunes, but everyone finds it delicious.

Soups

Inexpensive soups make inexpensive lunches. When eaten with whole-grain bread and some raw vegetable sticks, they are filling too. The "leavings" soup already mentioned is very inexpensive. So is split pea soup if you make your own and omit the ham. Put carrots, celery, and an onion in with the peas. Add thyme and a bayleaf and cook to a mush. I like navy bean soup cooked with only some onion bits and a tiny fragment of salt pork. I make a cheap corn chowder with salt pork, canned corn, and skim milk powder mixed thickly. I also make poor man's soup—potatoes sliced and boiled in water with a lump of margarine added. Take out a few potato slices and mash them with a fork to thicken this soup.

Potatoes

Potatoes are the cheapest vegetable you can eat—almost the cheapest food there is. When economizing on food, use a lot of potatoes. Boil and bake them with the skins; eat the skins. A baked potato topped with yogurt and cut-up onion tops is delicious. With margarine it has slightly more calories. With lemon juice it has less. When I peel potatoes for frying or mashing, I scrub them and peel them thickly, butter and bake the peelings and eat these with soup or salad instead of crackers or toast.

Meatless Meals

Since meat is probably the most expensive thing you buy, have meatless meals often. Use eggs and cheese, and make plant protein dishes and vegetable casseroles instead. If you add eggs, milk, protein bread crumbs, and cheese—or any combination of these—to a vegetable or vegetables, you don't need meat. Eat these casseroles with a slice or two of whole-grain bread, a few raw vegetables on the side, and a fruit and milk dessert. This is a balanced meal and sufficient for most older, not-too-active women. When using plant proteins in place of meat, combine a grain protein with a peanut or bean protein to get complete protein. For instance, a wheat and bean casserole is good protein, as is a peanut and bread crumb loaf.

TV Dinners

Don't buy TV dinners. You are paying for gravy and skimpy portions of overcooked vegetables. Freeze your leftovers in individual portions in the freezer. Wrap them in foil and heat these packages while you bake a potato and quick-cook a vegetable. I usually keep whole-wheat rolls in the refrigerator ready for baking or bran muffins or refrigerator biscuits on hand. I often make up large bowls of refrigerator salads so I can simply scoop out a portion on lettuce leaves. Cooking this way is as easy as eating TV dinners, and it's cheaper and much more healthful.

Sharing Meals

If you don't like to cook and eat by yourself, consider sharing—if you can find someone who shares your ideas about economical and healthful eating. This eliminates a lot of leftovers and adds some socialization to your life. I know four older women who live in the same building who get together to eat four nights a week. Each prepares a healthful, inexpensive meal for herself and the three others one night a week and "visits" on the remaining three nights.

I know another older woman who takes in several boarders every night. She prepares a healthful, inexpensive evening meal for three working girls who eat with her and pay her for the privilege. She charges them only enough to pay her entire grocery bill for the month.

If you don't wish to cook, investigate the Friendly Neighbor lunches for older people. Does your area have such a program? This is a federally subsidized lunch program for the elderly. You pay whatever you wish. I think you can eat much more healthfully at home, although I would not presume to knock a free—or practically free—program.

Fasting

Fast or near fast for a day occasionally when you've gained an unwanted pound or two or when your food money is running low. Have nothing but very diluted grapefruit juice during the day and a big reducer's milk shake for dinner. This is a day you really save money! I do this one day a week to keep my weight where I want it, but most people would not find this necessary.

Start Prepared

Don't start from scratch trying to live on a dollar a day. Start out with twenty extra dollars for staples—cereals and flours; shortening and oil; beans, rice, and split peas; a pound of sugar; some canned soups and juices; canned fruits, vegetables, and seasonings; coffee and tea; and margarine and skim milk powder.

In fact, if food prices continue to rise—as they most certainly will—it may be necessary to spend one's "extra" money for these staples every month or two.

9.

Dressing Nicely on Ten Dollars a Month

Clothes do not make the man—or the woman—but they help. First impressions are based largely upon the way we look—our grooming and our clothes. Many people who live on very limited incomes look dowdy or shabby and definitely out of style. But they don't need to. They either don't spend their money wisely, or they spend what little money they have on everything but clothes, which I think is a big mistake. Nice clothes are good for the morale; they lift the spirits and make you feel good about yourself.

If you plan your wardrobe carefully and take care of it, it doesn't take much money to dress attractively. It does take a little, of course. But almost everyone can squeeze ten dollars a month for clothes out of a Social Security check. That's what I spend, and I have clothes nice looking enough for

every occasion, as many as I need, and I go a good bit, to
all kinds of places, among all kinds of people.

Two of Everything Is Enough

When you are not working, you don't need many clothes.
Two of everything is enough if these two outfits look smart
and are appropriate and comfortable. I learned this when I
traveled through Europe and Asia for a year shortly after my
retirement. I had two of everything—two pants, two jackets,
two blouses, two tops, two dresses (one long and one short),
one pair of walking shoes, and one pair of dress shoes. I wore
a travel coat and took a crocheted stole, and I found that with
these few clothes I could be appropriately dressed for every
occasion. Everything went together; everything was washable;
everything was comfortable and constructed of sturdy, long-
wearing fabrics that lasted through the year.

When I came home, I started to plan my entire wardrobe
with the same care I had used to select my travel clothes.
Now I plan my wardrobe at least two years in advance, keeping in mind where I'm going to go, what I'm going to do,
what clothes I have that I'll still be wearing, and what re-
placements I'll need.

Begin by Cleaning Out the Closet

Every season I go through my closet and discard everything that has grown ugly and shabby or completely out of
date. I hate wearing ugly old shabby clothes, even around the
house or in the garden. They make me feel ugly and shabby
and old—and poor. A neat pair of denim pants and a T-shirt
and vest, a crisp tailored housecoat, or a cotton skirt and
blouse are appropriate for house and garden—not a left-over
Sunday dress that was pretty five or six years ago but has
been worn and washed to a faded and depressing dowdiness.
These clothes should be discarded and not left to hang and
clutter a closet. Everything in the closet should be sparkling
clean, ready to wear, and as updated as possible.

How to Plan a Wardrobe

When you plan your wardrobe, think of everything you're going to do and everywhere you're going to go, and then plan clothes appropriate for every occasion.

For instance, I spend a lot of time in the country. I like to hike, garden, sunbathe, and swim, and I need neat, casual clothes—denim pants, cotton jackets, a cap, a sun hat, a swim suit, and a coverup. One friend of mine who is a joiner of women's clubs and groups and who goes out almost every afternoon and evening needs no casual clothes such as I have at all. She needs dressier dresses and a few clothes to wear around the house.

Begin your wardrobe planning by going through what you already have that can be worn during the coming season. Try everything on with the shoes, stockings, underwear, and accessories you plan to wear with it. Look at yourself with a very critical eye. Note repairs needed and other changes that could be made to keep yourself current, and look for any refitting or making over that needs to be done. Take care of these things first, and try to think of ways to extend your present wardrobe. Be creative. Make a list of odds and ends and inexpensive items that would bring your present wardrobe up-to-date and make it more adaptable and attractive. The chances are, you'll need only a few new clothes once you accomplish this creative refurbishing.

Then make a list of new garments you must have and, again, plan carefully and creatively. Separates that can be worn together and with what you already have are usually a good idea when money is limited. So is choosing the new things in colors that go with your present major accessories —the shoes, purses, gloves, and costume jewelry you have on hand.

The Secret Is Sewing

I question whether anyone can be well dressed on ten dollars a month unless she sews. How well you sew will determine how well you look. This was a preparation I made for retirement. I invested in a secondhand, featherweight portable sewing machine and started to sew. (If I had done this years ago when I was young, I could have saved myself thousands of dollars and been better dressed as well.) I paid fifty dollars for the machine, and it has paid for itself a hundred times over, since I make not only my clothes but everything for the house and for gifts as well.

Choosing a Machine

I don't recommend for the novice one of those expensive, fabulous cabinet machines. I think all that machinery is frightening, and if you find you don't enjoy sewing, the thing just sits there and makes you feel guilty every time you look at it. It's much better for us older ones to try out our sewing skills with a little, inexpensive machine that's easier to maneuver than the high-powered ones. Those great machines are for a young person who is going to do a lot of sewing for a family, a young person who has the potential for becoming an expert seamstress.

Most of us who start to sew late in life are not going to become all that expert. However, I have found that you do not need to be an expert to make good-looking clothes if you choose your patterns carefully, select materials that are easy to sew, and get your figure into some semblance of shape so that it's easy to fit.

Learning to Sew

Anyone can learn to sew. Simple sewing requires no great skill. I began my sewing stint with an easy-to-sew housecoat pattern, an inexpensive piece of material, and an illustrated book on beginning sewing from the library. I studied the book, then did exactly what the pattern instructions told me to, and my first garment was a complete success. If you don't like the idea of teaching yourself from a book and the illustrated instructions that come with the pattern, you can take lessons at night school or at a sewing machine place.

Sewing is easy these days, much easier than it used to be, with press-on interfacing, iron-on tape, ballpoint machine needles, pinking shears, Velcro fastenings, and all the other things that make the task quick and easy and pleasant. A good clerk in the fabric store can inform and help with these selections. I've a favorite clerk who practically gives me a free lesson in sewing every time I buy a piece of material.

Patterns are much simpler than they used to be, too. All the major pattern companies now feature some simple patterns. There are Sew-and-Go patterns, Jiffy patterns, Easy-to-Sew patterns, Make-It-Tonight-and-Wear-It-Tomorrow patterns. These are patterns that have only three or four pieces to be seamed together without zippers or buttonholes or other difficult and tricky construction.

They look better on slim people, of course, and they are always pictured on the young—as is everything else in the pattern books—but old women can wear them too, if they are sufficiently shapely. There are patterns that come in two sizes in the same envelope and you can make the top in one size and the bottom in a larger size, good news for pear-shaped people. There are even teaching patterns that teach you to sew.

Although I have been sewing for quite some time now and thoroughly enjoy it, I do not have the aptitude to become an expert. So I avoid patterns with set-in pockets, bound buttonholes and lapels, and tricky collars—things that make a garment look tacky and home-made if you don't do them expertly. I avoid materials with stripes and plaids and big checks, also soft sleazy materials that have to be hand basted and sewn with great care, materials that require a garment to be lined, and bulky materials that are hard to work with.

Selecting and Adapting Patterns

I have no trouble finding patterns that I know I can sew. When I find one that looks well on me, I use it over and over, making adaptations as I have learned to do. This saves money, as most patterns cost from one to three or four dollars. It saves time too. When a pattern has been used and fitted previously, you don't need to spend time measuring and fitting and figuring out how the pieces go together. All you do the second and subsequent times is cut it out and sew it.

I have used my first housecoat pattern at least fifty times. I've made housecoats, shirts, jackets, blouses, jumpers, and raincoats from it. I have an overblouse pattern that I have used forever, and I will be making blouses from this pattern when I am ninety if I should live so long. It fits perfectly and cuts well from a small amount of material—important when you consider the cost of material these days.

I look through the pattern books every season, and, when I see a pattern that's just my type, I buy it. I buy patterns before I buy material so I'll know how much material I need when I find just the right piece. To be sure of the fit, I make up the pattern using an old sheet or some very inexpensive material. I am not sufficiently expert to cut into good material until I have first worked over a pattern to achieve a perfect fit, which is essential if a garment is to look smart. Any good book on home sewing will show and tell you how to check the fit of a pattern and show and tell you what to do to make the pattern fit your particular figure.

Age Has Nothing to Do with Learning to Sew

In my last sewing class—a course in tailoring—there was an eighty-two-year-old woman making her second garment, a jacket that came out beautifully. (I was learning to make T-shirts with turtle necks.) I have a seventy-year-old friend who went to school and learned what is known as the Bishop method of sewing, and she now makes for herself and her daughters chic and lovely clothes that look as if they came from the most expensive and exclusive shops.

Why Sew?

The advantages of home sewing are many, especially for us poor and older ones. The clothes last longer than bought clothes. They're better sewn, better finished, and fit better than the moderately priced clothes most of us can afford. Most important, you can have exactly the kind of clothes you want. It's almost impossible to find a finished garment in the color you need, in a style that suits you, and in the kind of easy-care material you want. Most people know the kind of clothes they'd like to have, the kind they look well in, and the kind that are comfortable; when you sew, you can have those kinds of clothes.

For instance, I want long sleeves, even in summer, to cover my obscene-looking elbows. I want an overblouse to come down over my hipline and hide my thick middle. I like dresses that hang straight from the shoulder for the same reason. I like blouses with ruffles around the neck, or that have a stand-up collar, or that tie in a bow to hide my under-the-chin wattles. I like six-gore skirts that enable me to step easily in and out of buses and boats and airplanes. I like pants that fit, with a zipper at the waist and with deep hems I can let down when they shrink. I like matching sleeveless jackets that come to just the right length on my hipline. I want denim housecoats and fragile looking caftans that wear like iron. I want only washable materials. I want separates that go with everything I have. I want colors that blend with my basic color scheme. I want all this for ten dollars a month. You can't possibly have it unless you sew.

There are always scraps from which to make caps and purses and belts and ties and all kinds of accessories, another advantage of home sewing. I get ideas for these things from pictures in magazines and handcraft shops and things seen in department and clothing stores when I look-shop. I can usually cut my own patterns for these things now that I have plenty of time to experiment. By adding your own touches of embroidery, appliqué, lace, braid, and other creative trim and designs, you can make your simple, inexpensive clothes look much more expensive than they are.

Long-Range Planning a Must

I plan my clothes at least two years in advance and write down my plan. This is so that when I see an inexpensive material I like, I can buy it and keep it on hand until needed. Being well dressed on practically nothing starts with a plan and a list. When you know what you'll need a year from now, you can bargain-shop from now until then. I always carry my plan in my purse so I'll know how much material I need for a garment when I find just the right piece.

This is how a two-year plan looks; this is how a home-made wardrobe is put together for practically pennies.

Spring and Summer Wardrobe

New Things to Make and Things to Do	Cost of Material
Pink caftan	
3 yards of 45-inch material at $3.50	$10.50
(Have lace and trimming)	
Purple and lavender print 2-piece bathing suit	
1 yard of 60-inch material at $4.00	4.00
Orange polyester pants	
1¼-yard remnant	4.00
Orange and bone figured sleeveless jacket	
¾-yard of 60-inch material at $4.00	3.00
Puff purse out of scraps of these two	
fabrics with bit of green added	——
Bone evening blouse fixed over to wear with this suit—	
make collar and tie from tail—repair bone jewelry	——
Belt for above suit—bone belting and buckle	1.85
Green polyester pants	
1½-yard remnant	3.50
Wear with white lace blouse,	
make tie for blouse from green pants goods	——
Green and white print blouse	
with bow tie from print left from evening dress	——

Wear with white crocheted jacket vest,
wash and reblock and shorten   ———
Crochet white belt for green pants
from scraps of yarn on hand, wrap cardboard buckle   ———
Puff purse out of scraps of green pants and print top   ———
Long green and white polyester print evening dress
   3½ yards of 60-inch material at $1.20   4.20
Wear with white crocheted stole—
put green cross-stitch on ends—have yarn   ———
Evening bag from scraps   ———
Faded shoes dyed green to match
evening dress—dye for shoes   1.45
Sequins and beads to make earrings and pendant
for evening dress   2.00
Pink polka dot blouse to wear with denim pants—
from scraps bought at garage sale   .25
Reversible denim cap and purse to wear with
denim pants—from scraps of denim and pink material   ———
Buckle for belt to wear with denim pants—
belt braided from denim scraps   .85
Coverup
   2½ yards of 45-inch material at $1.20   3.00
Bone shoes with T-straps
to wear with the pants suits or dresses   25.00
Knee-hi stockings, 4 pair   1.00

By sewing, by making over, and by using scraps for accessories, I was able to get the new spring and summer clothes I needed for approximately seventy dollars—about what one would have to pay for one bought pants suit.

Fall and Winter

New Things to Make	*Cost of Material*
Blue polyester pants	
1¼ yards of 60-inch material	$5.00
Two blue T-shirts with turtle neck tops	
1½ yards at $2.98	4.50
(Have tops and jackets to wear with these)	
Dark blue and white print blouse with tie	
1¼ yards of 60-inch material at $2.98	3.75
Travel cap to wear with dark blue travel coat	
¼ yard light blue suede cloth at $8.90	2.25
Dark blue piping	.75
(Have material for lining)	
Red walking shoes to wear with either black or navy pants	25.00

Crocheted sweater-vests to wear with navy pants
and T-shirts, in navy, coral, and white—
have navy and coral yarn, need one skein of white   1.25
New buttons for red shirt   1.00

Making and following a plan such as the above eliminates impulse shopping as well as the need to rush out and buy something to wear for special occasions. When you wait until the last minute to shop, you usually come home with something that will do, but that does not do anything for you. If you would be smartly dressed on very little money, never buy anything that will do—buy only things that do something for you.

If You Don't Sew or Don't Want To

If you don't sew and don't want to learn or have tried and don't enjoy it, shop for bargains at end-of-season sales, special sales, and wholesale houses. I have a friend who buys one basic outfit a year, as nice as she can afford, and wears it everywhere. She fills in with a few little odds and ends from mail order houses and discount stores and thrift shops.

If you can find a good thrift shop, a place where the wealthy and chic dispose of their cast-off clothes, you are in luck. I know a woman who does volunteer work at a thrift shop set up by the Junior League just so she'll have first chance at some of the better clothes brought in by these young matrons, many of whom have exquisite and expensive taste in clothes.

Buying Coats

Don't economize on coats. The $120 a year that I spend on clothes does not include coats or the good leather purses that I like. These I get with my "gift money." I let it be known frankly and audibly that I prefer money for Mother's Day, Christmas, and birthday gifts. I let this gift money accumulate, and every three or four years, I buy the best-looking coat I can afford and a good-looking leather bag. It pays to put your money in a coat because you wear a coat almost two-thirds of the year. People see you first and most often in a coat. They get an impression of you and your clothes from the coat. Therefore, economize on other things, but not on a coat or a purse. Get the most beautiful coat you can possibly afford. Wear the simple little homemade dress, which most people will never see, beneath it. The simple little homemade dress is beautiful too, of course, because it's much easier to make than a coat.

Crocheting

Crochet is something else that a person with a limited clothes budget ought to know about. Even a beginner can make sweaters, stoles, vests, and little odds and ends to add variety and color and warmth to a wardrobe. There is almost no limit to the things that experienced, expert crocheters can make.

Teaching Yourself to Crochet

If you don't already crochet, there are little books for beginners that will enable you to learn to chain and to do single and double crochet and other simple stitches. If you wish, you can take a course in crochet and learn to follow simple patterns and directions—many times you can get help from relatives and friends.

However, there are some things you can make from single crochet alone that are quick, easy, warm, and nice. Single crochet is a cinch—anybody can do that, and it's rather fun; you just do the same stitch over and over. You can pick it up and do it without thinking, any time, any place. Belts, stoles, and necklace ties are three of my favorites.

Yarn is not expensive. You can often find it on sale for less than a dollar a skein. It's washable, and you can block these simple things yourself with a steam iron and a make-shift press cloth.

What Goes On Underneath

Nothing makes you feel richer than beautiful underwear. You don't have to be rich, though, if you make your own. Making lingerie is not difficult once you tailor a pattern to fit your figure. The garments you make yourself last for years if you select the materials wisely, wash them carefully, and keep them in exquisite repair. Color is important, too. White things tend to get yellow or grey with age. With white skirts or slacks you almost have to wear white. But beige or black and pale pastels are more practical colors and will stay beautiful much longer.

Where to Buy Inexpensive Underwear

When you are thin, you can buy the little light-weight garments from the dime and discount stores and mail order houses. (Being thin has many advantages, among them the fact that it's much cheaper to clothe yourself attractively.) Trying bras and girdles on for fit is absolutely necessary, so if there's no place to try them on, don't buy them. If a bra or girdle doesn't fit perfectly and feel comfortable, it's no bargain.

These inexpensive garments will wear longer if washed by hand in cool or tepid water after every wearing, so you need no more than two of everything. The same is true of panty hose. If you rinse them out every night, little or no soap is necessary, and they last much longer.

Extending the Life of Your Underwear

Bedraggled, tattle-tale grey underwear, like hose with runs, should be discarded. But sometimes it is possible to extend the life of a garment with new straps, a new hook and eye piece, or an extender from the dime store. Some white garments can be bleached or whitened. Bleach should not be used on elasticized material, however. Some materials can be tinted. Have the garment wet and unfolded when tinting so that it does not spot. Beige is a good color to try on a yellowed undergarment. However, some fabrics do not take dye well, if at all.

Undergarments Are Important

The right kind of undergarments make a big difference in how you look on the outside. For instance, under a sheer dress, a slip with lace on the bottom lets your knees show through. Very unattractive! Wear slips without lace at the bottom with these dresses.

The right shade of stocking is important. Try on different shades with each dress to see what shade looks best. Sheer, lightweight, long-leg pants liners look much better under pants than the shorties that leave a line and show where they stop. There are also garterless, long-leg pants girdles that are seamed and shaped to give us older ones a better looking behind in pants. There are bras designed to lift a sagging bosom to a shapelier, more youthful appearance. There are bras made especially for T-shirts, and if you wear T-shirts without a vest or jacket—you probably shouldn't—try on some of these too.

Buy your underwear with the same care that you use to buy your other clothes. You can't afford *any* failures. I have a friend who shops carefully for outer garments, but she buys underwear haphazardly and quickly—girdles that don't keep her where she belongs, bras that don't fit, slips too long or too short, and off-shade stockings. These keep her from looking as well as she should.

It is attention to many small details that spells the difference between looking good and looking great. Now that you have the time, you might as well look great.

10.

How to Look Nice on Nearly Nothing — Penny Grooming

When one is old, grooming is important. The young can get away with casualness, but we older ones don't have the face, the figure, and the style to carry it off. We look frankly terrible with unkempt hair, sloppy housedresses, and shapeless shoes.

I once had a friend who lived in an apartment house for the indigent elderly. A stale, overpowering oder permeated the halls and elevator—the clinging smell of unwashed heads and bodies in need of bathing and of clothes worn too long without washing and cleaning—a smell I still associate with age and poverty.

It is not necessary to spend much money to be meticulously groomed and fresh—all it takes is time and effort, a few odds and ends from the dime store and the cut-rate drugstore, some poor-people know-how, and a persistent resolve. It isn't the kind of cosmetics one uses, it is the consistency with which one uses them, and we now have time to use them consistently and to care for ourselves properly.

When you know you're looking as pretty as possible, you feel much better than if you're slopping around in an ugly old robe and hair that hasn't been washed for three weeks. Appearance makes a tremendous difference in the way you feel about yourself and the way you react to others—and in the way they react to you.

Do not believe all the cosmetics advertising you see on television and in the magazines. People pay exorbitant prices for packaging, fragrance, and clever advertising; they spend many dollars needlessly every year for expensive cosmetics that are no better than those from the dime store, the cut-rate drugstore, or the kitchen cupboard.

Lanolin, the All-Purpose Cosmetic

There is a limit to what creams, emollients, and moisturizers can do for any skin. They soften and lubricate. They do not firm and remove wrinkles already there, as some advertisements claim. It is foolish to spend money on products so advertised. An excellent, homemade, inexpensive cosmetic can be made from lanolin and petroleum jelly. Because it is inexpensive, it can be used lavishly and regularly on face, neck, hands, nails, feet, and the entire body. It softens, smooths, and, in my opinion, is a marvelous all-purpose cream.

If you'd like to try it, this is the way. Get a one-pound jar of lanolin from the drugstore. It will cost you around four dollars, but it is still a bargain because a little goes a long way. Be sure to get the hydrous type that will mix with water. Also, get a one-pound jar of petroleum jelly for about a dollar. Measure a cup of petroleum jelly and a half cup of lanolin into a small pan and heat them slowly until they're melted and mixed. Pour the cream into jars. This will last quite some time and will be the only cream you need. It will be necessary to get a second pound of petroleum jelly later to use with the rest of the lanolin.

An actress friend of mine used to pay twenty dollars for a salt and lanolin rub, which she said made her skin glow. You can give yourself one for twenty cents or less, and it does make skin glow, even old, dry, beat-up skin. Rub the lanolin jelly mix onto yourself—face, neck, elbows, and your entire body. Then massage yourself mightily with table salt, concentrating on the scruffy spots and fatty lumps until you are nicely pink all over.

Then get under a warm shower and wash the mess off. Don't use any soap. Use a body brush if you have one. The warm water will take off the salt and most of the lanolin but not quite all of it. Enough will stay on your skin to soften and lubricate, but not enough to soil clothing or sheets. Try this treatment twice weekly. It will make your skin look and feel younger, fresher, and smoother.

Rather than using this cream at night, because it is rather greasy, I spread a light film on my face and neck every morning and leave it on while I'm having breakfast and straightening the house. It does the same thing as an expensive overnight cream—softens and smooths.

Also use this mixture for cuticle cream. Apply to the nails three or four times a day, then push cuticle back with a towel. Resist the impulse to treat cuticle roughly; use the lanolin and towel treatment instead. You can also use it on feet and toenails. Wear bedsocks or use it in the morning with house socks when you cream your face.

Other Inexpensive and "Kitchen" Cosmetics

Perhaps the inexpensive or "kitchen" cosmetics that I think are good won't suit your tastes exactly, but experiment until you find something that suits you. You don't need expensive cosmetics to be exquisitely groomed.

I think soap is bad for aging skins and use very little of it. If you shower daily in warm water, soap isn't necessary. Also, I seldom buy Kleenex—I tear off little pieces of toilet paper and stuff them in the Kleenex box. Never spend money on things you don't really need.

I clean my face every night with a cheap, deep-pore cleanser

that I get at the cut-rate drugstore. I rub it in well, and, instead of tissuing off, I wash it off with hot water. Some people
prefer a mild soap for cleaning, of course.

Canned lemon juice put in an empty bottle and diluted
with a bit of water serves as an excellent freshener both night
and morning. Lemon juice supposedly restores the acid balance of your skin. Some people use witch hazel from the drug
store as a freshener.

A homemade toothpaste that really does whiten and brighten
teeth can be used occasionally. Take a pinch of salt and a
pinch of soda, and moisten them with a few drops of canned
lemon juice.

I make ordinary toothpaste last twice as long by using only
a tiny dot on the brush. The same is true of shampoo. Since
I wash my hair every four or five days, I use only one capful
of the herbal essence shampoo I buy at the dime store. I wash
only once—two sudsings are not necessary—and rinse until
it squeaks, an indication that hair is clean and rinsed sufficiently.

I occasionally use a color rinse—a few drops of whitener
—which costs an extra dollar at the beauty parlor, but only a
few cents when you use it yourself at home.

I find makeup foundation tends to stick in wrinkles and
makes me look cakey. So I buy some good, inexpensive hand
lotion, pour it into a dispenser, and add a bit of glycerin
from the cut-rate drugstore. I apply this generously, let it
dry thoroughly, then give my face a light dusting of powder.
I used to pay six to ten dollars a box for blended powder, but
I like the kind I mix myself just as well. I buy dime store
powder in two shades and mix a darker blend in summer and
lighter in winter, to match my skin tone.

I use blusher, also from the dime store, put on with a
brush, blending it and using it sparingly. I then use a powder
brush to brush powder out of creases and an eyebrow pencil
to even up my brows. A bit of powdered eye shadow and a
pale pink or coral lipstick—all from the dime store—finish

off my face. Most older women should avoid bright reds, reds with blue or wine in them, cream lipsticks that run, and those that have a frosted look. These make us look older than we are.

I use an inexpensive talcum powder and matching spray cologne in place of perfume. I buy roll-on deodorant—any kind that's cheap—and use it daily. However, if you don't perspire freely, you can make your own deodorant by mixing a tablespoon of talcum powder or cornstarch with three tablespoons of baking soda. Keep this in a little dish and dab on with cotton balls. Many people find this deodorizes sufficiently.

I don't use dime-store nail polish. I think the more expensive kinds are better, go on more easily, and last longer. I like to put on nail polish with a tiny camel's hair water color brush bought from the art supply store. It's so much easier to manage than the brush that's in the bottle. My manicurist used this kind of brush, and I can do a more professional-looking job with it; it's well worth the money because it lasts forever. To clean it, I dip it into a bottle of dime-store polish remover. I use polish only occasionally. At other times I groom my nails with a buffer and some cornstarch mixed with shavings from a pumice stone, also from the dime store.

Excess hair in your nose or on your lip or chin is ugly and should be removed. Apparently, age and lack of estrogen promote the growth of hair in inappropriate places. To keep myself hair free, I use an ordinary razor and a tweezers and a special little "nose trimming" scissors I bought from a mail order house. Some people like a depilatory but it's more expensive than shaving, tweezing, and clipping, also smellier and messier.

Besides these, an emory board or two, an orange stick, a comb and brush, and rollers to roll up hair are everything one really needs. A hair dryer is almost essential when you do your own hair and, in the long run, a tremendous saving. Once you have the tools for grooming, they last forever and one has to purchase only one or two of the cosmetic items every month or so.

Grooming Routine a Necessity

Not only does one need the tools for grooming, one needs a routine: an every-five-days routine, an every-night routine, and an every-morning routine. I find this difficult, but I do look better when I follow a routine regularly. Every morning I inspect myself in my inexpensive full-length mirror and try to look as if I were going out to lunch with chic and wealthy friends, even when I'm not.

Money or the lack of it has little to do with the way one looks. It's choice, know-how, time, and effort. It's easier, of course, if you go to the hairdresser's every week and let the manicurist and the pedicurist take over your hands and feet and have a sauna and a paid-for massage, but you don't need to. You can look almost as well without them.

Hair—Your Crowning Glory

I heard someone say recently that if your hair looks great, you look good all over, and if your hair doesn't look good, it doesn't make any difference what else you do to yourself. This is especially true if you are older. Unkempt, old hair looks very bad indeed.

If you get your hair done at the beauty parlor every week, three or four permanents a year and five or six cuts, you'll be spending $400 or $500 a year on hair alone; and if you have it colored, the cost will run up to $700 or $800. This is more than most of us can or wish to spend for good-looking hair.

If you are living on a limited budget, you simply cannot afford to have your hair colored at a salon. It's difficult to do a good hair color job at home, and grey is better than a poor color job. Grey hair does make one look older—there is no question about that—but who cares? Grey hair can be soft and pretty; it goes with our faces and the rest of us and blends us with our age.

If you need only a rinse to blend in a little grey, that is another thing. You can give yourself a rinse at home for pennies. A rinse can also take the yellow out of white or grey hair and make it look softer and more silvery, but don't make your hair too dark or blue or purple. Dark blue or purple hair shrieks age and lack of chic.

I know a woman who washes her own hair every week in the shower, puts on a rinse, puts on a scarf and dashes down the street to the beauty school, where she gets a beautiful set and comb-out for a couple of dollars. The students spend a great deal of time brushing and combing and strive to make each head look superb before the supervisor examines their work. She does not care for their shampoos and she saves the price of a rinse by putting it on herself.

Some schools reduce their rates even further on certain days of the week for senior citizens. When going to a school, ask for an operator in her last few months of schooling and make an appointment with the same girl each time. Ask her to recommend someone when she graduates. A little tip to the operator is not mandatory but keeps her in a pleasant state of mind.

How can you keep your hair looking nice if you can't afford to go to the beauty parlor every week? One alternative is to let it grow and wear it long, if you are one of the lucky ones who can. Beautiful white or grey hair done on top of the head, wound around in braids, or worn severely with a bun at the neck make these women stand out in a crowd, and they need spend nothing at all on their hair. Another alternative is to have hair cut short, wear it uncurled, and wash and dry it yourself, perhaps with a blow dryer. This is easy, but few older women look their best with this short, easy-to-care-for hair either. Those who do look distinctive and chic. This kind of hair usually requires cutting once a month, so you do have to go to the beauty parlor occasionally.

Another alternative is to wear a wig, and some older women wear a wig all the time. If you have poor or thinning hair, a becoming, easy-to-care-for wig may be the solution to your hair problem. Select a wig carefully, then have it expertly trimmed and styled to suit you. If you learn to wash and care for a wig yourself, there's no more expense. People tell me they get so used to a wig they can wear it all the time and never know they have it on.

Sometimes you can find beautiful wigs on sale for about half the regular price. If you can find one that suits you exactly, that is the time to get it, but a cheap wig that doesn't do anything for you is no bargain.

Doing Your Own Hair

Wigs make me feel frankly phoney; I'm more comfortable with my own hair. I like it blowing in the wind, unscarved. I like it brushed and shining and finger-combed. I tried both long hair and short hair and didn't like the way I looked with either, so I was forced to compromise and spend just a little money to keep my hair looking acceptable.

I get two or three permanents a year, have a cut or two between permanents, and wash, rinse, and set my own. I've learned to roll my own hair on rollers. By the second day it's impossible to tell whether the beauty operator or I did my hair.

Time spent under the dryer is not wasted. I give myself a manicure and pedicure while I'm drying. My hair looks neat and casual, and I can let it blow in the wind and then brush it until it shines silvery. A hairnet worn at night shapes it to my head.

A Hairnet That Lasts

To make this hairnet, cut a circle of nylon net or tulle about twenty inches in diameter. Turn up an inch all around the circle and sew this hem in place on the sewing machine. A quarter of an inch below your first stitching, make another row of stitching and run a piece of tiny, round elastic through this casing, leading the elastic through with a small safety pin. Gather the cap comfortably to fit your head, and sew the elastic ends firmly together. When the elastic stretches, remove it and run in a fresh piece.

Giving Yourself a Dry Shampoo

Talcum powder keeps your head smelling fresh. If you are one of those who get your hair done only every two weeks in order to save money and you want to freshen between shampoos, a bit of talcum powder will make your head smell better and clean your scalp. Old heads washed only every two weeks will smell. Perhaps you can't smell your own head, but others can.

I used to think I had to buy a can of dry shampoo, but I found that I could use nice-smelling talcum which I buy in a big can from the dime store to do the same thing. The powder costs about a fourth as much as the shampoo and lasts ten times as long. Don't use this if your hair is not grey, however, because traces of unremoved powder will show in dark hair.

To give yourself the dry shampoo, part your hair with your fingers, shake powder over your head, and rub it in well, then brush it out. Keep brushing until all obvious traces of powder are removed. This removes the stale smell from scalp and makes hair look softer and whiter.

I used to know a lovely old lady who never washed her hair all winter long. She thought a shampoo would give her a cold. She mixed talcum with coarse white cornmeal and rubbed that into her head every few days and spent a long time brushing it out. In the summer she washed her head with a beaten egg and rain water with a few drops of bluing added. She had thick, beautiful, snow-white hair which she wore braided and coiled on top of her head, truly her crowning glory. She didn't spend a cent on her hair.

Hands, Nails and Manicuring

How do you want your hands to look? Personally, I like plain, useful-looking old hands with short, neat, natural nails. I dislike old hands with long, brightly polished, salon-perfect fingernails, but many people like them. Either way, you can learn to fix your nails yourself. For both the glamorous and the no-nonsense approach, the basics are the same: some simple home hand care and a manicure you give yourself twice weekly—a bit simpler than those you pay six dollars for at the salon, but almost as good.

1. Remove polish with polish remover, then, with the fine side of an emory board, file nails from side to center in the shape you want them. If your nails are ridged and tend to break and split, short nails are best.
2. Massage some of the lanolin-vaseline mix well into your hands and nails, then add some pumice powder. (You can shave this powder from your dime-store pumice stone into a little dish. If you use a kitchen knife for the shaving and hold it properly, you can sharpen the knife as you shave.) Work this pumice into the cuticle and push back the cuticle gently. Don't try to cut your own cuticle.
3. Scrub your hands in warm soapy water, using a little brush if you have one, and push the cuticle back with a towel.
4. Buff your nails to give them the stimulation they need. Buffing increases circulation and tends to encourage healthy growth. If you buff for finish and gloss, use corn-starch mixed with a bit of the pumice in another little dish. Dip the end of the buffer into the powdered mix and stroke each nail in the direction away from you, not back and forth, until nails are pink and shiny. Don't overdo it—too much friction and pumice can damage your nails. Pumice tends to make the ridges on old nails less noticeable, but too much buffing will take off the surface of the nails. When finished with buffing, wipe your nails with a clean towel and use hand lotion.
5. If applying polish, you really should use a base coat first, then two coats of polish and a sealer, and let your nails dry between coats, which will take the good part of

half a day. However, I find that if you give yourself the above easy-to-do manicure twice a week, two coats of well-applied polish alone will suffice. Apply polish by using three clean strokes of the brush on each nail. Dip the brush into the bottle of remover before dipping it into the polish. Do your right hand first if you are right-handed, then do your left, then repeat the process. You can learn to do a good job of applying polish, but it does take a bit of practice if you've never done it before.

One manicure a week may suffice if you apply a thin, touch-up coat of polish in the middle of the week. If you don't have time to dry the touch up, take off all the polish and buff. Unpolished nails look better than those with chipped, worn polish.

Protective care is especially important for old hands. If you want really nice hands, get yourself some rubber gloves to wear when doing major cleanups and dirty work. If your nails are brittle, get a small bottle of olive oil from the super-market, pour it into a little pan, heat it slightly, and soak your nails in this three or four times a week.

Brown spots and prominent veins indicate that you have been around for quite some time and have managed to sur-vive. A dermatologist can remove these spots if they bother you and you can afford it.

What to Do About Your Face

After all these years, most of us have learned to live with our faces as they are, and now we simply do the best we can by them, which means we cleanse and lubricate and remove hair where it is not supposed to be, and make them up as lightly and attractively as possible.

Everyone has her own ideas about cleansing and cream-ing. The thing to do is to do it consistently and not be taken in by ridiculous advertising. You cannot remove sags and wrinkles already there with creams or massage or facial exercises. Some of the sagging and wrinkling might have been prevented or partially prevented by one or more of these things if you had done them earlier, though this too is controversial.

Wrinkles and sag can be removed or improved with a face-lift. Many women in moderate circumstances, as well as richer ones, now have their faces lifted, but it is not financially feasible for many of us.

When someone advised a noted, aging author on a television show that she should have her face lifted, she responded that her lines and wrinkles were indications that she had both lived and loved. Her face was the result of a full and complete life—interesting, exciting, and sometimes sad. So it is with all of us. A face-lift does not last indefinitely. Further aging takes place, and in time one ends up lined and sagging again; then touch-up surgery is necessary.

Texture Can Be Improved

With proper care, the texture of skin can be improved, no matter what one's age. Masques and deep pore cleaning *do* help. Things that people put on their faces years ago, before the advent of expensive cosmetics, included cucumbers, strawberries, honey, cream, milk, egg white, lemon juice, and oatmeal. These things probably do your skin as much good as the expensive cosmetics currently sold over the counter.

The masque I like best, because I always have the ingredients on hand and because it does seem to soften and tighten temporarily, is an egg white–oatmeal masque. I beat up an egg white, not too stiff, add a bit of oatmeal to make it the right consistency for spreading, put it on my face and neck and let dry for about a half hour, then wash it off with warm water and finish with lemon juice mixed with water.

Other kitchen masques are used by some of my beautiful, older friends. When you have some of these ingredients on hand, you may want to try them.

1. Beat the yolk of an egg, add some skim milk powder and half a peeled, mashed, ripe avocado, and beat well to mix. Dip a wad of cotton into the avocado cream and dab your face with it. Continue to apply until boredom sets in, then finish with a splash of water and lemon juice.
2. In a blender, put half a cucumber cut in pieces, an egg white, and a tablespoon of skim milk powder, and blend until smooth. Apply to your face and neck, and let it remain for thirty minutes. Wash off and finish with lemon juice.
3. Mash several strawberries until you have two teaspoons of pulp and juice. Blend in two teaspoons of vegetable oil. Smooth the mixture onto your face and neck and massage it in well. Let it remain as a masque for ten minutes, then rinse off with warm water, and finish with lemon juice.
4. Add an egg yolk to two tablespoons of heavy cream. Beat until mixed. Beat the egg white to a froth and stir into the first mixture. Apply a hot, wet washcloth to your face until the pores are open, then massage the egg and cream mixture well into the skin. Let dry. Wash off with warm water and finish with lemon juice.

The quantities suggested should make enough for two or three masques; keep them covered in the refrigerator, and you can use them two or three days in a row. I personally believe it does not make much difference which of these good things you put on your skin; the fact that you are doing *something* to it tends to make old skin look fresher.

Deep-Pore Cleansing

For thorough cleansing once or twice a week, you may want to try a Swiss Kriss facial herbal sauna, which makes your face feel very fresh and clean. Swiss Kriss is a herbal laxative, and you can buy it at most drugstores for about $2.25 a package, which lasts quite some time.

Put about two quarts of water in a pan on the stove and bring it to a boil, add one heaping teaspoon of the Swiss Kriss, turn off the heat, and let the mixture brew for several minutes. Remove from heat and put the pan in the sink. Put on a shower cap to save your hair, and put a big towel over both your head and the pan. Close your eyes and steam your face for about five minutes, turning face from side to side and breathing from the side of the towel. Rub your face briskly with a dry towel, and finish off with lemon juice and water.

Gaylord Hauser, the health and beauty expert, recommended this facial. He says, in his inimitable way, that a millionairess could not buy a better skin purge, and we can do it in our own little kitchenette sinks. Hauser recommends using pure vegetable oil on skin, rather than other creams; he says many of the creams are loaded with wax, which clogs and enlarges the pores.

A good night cream containing vegetable oil is made as follows. Melt together over heat two tablespoons of hydrous type lanolin and a half cup of whatever unsaturated vegetable oil you have on hand, then beat in three tablespoons of witch hazel. Spread on in a thin film at night.

For a Beautiful Smell

1. Take a daily shower and use talcum powder that matches the cologne you use.

2. Put on fresh underwear every day. Get in the habit of rinsing your stockings and underwear nightly.

3. Wash outer clothing as needed and have coats, jackets, and suits cleaned as often as necessary. Try to eliminate clothes that need dry cleaning because this is expensive.

4. Use underarm deodorant or the soda-talcum mix every day.

5. Clean your teeth night and morning and after eating; clean your tongue and mouth, and use floss. Pay especial attention to dentures.

6. Wash your hair often; give yourself a dry shampoo between washings if needed.

7. Put talcum powder in your shoes when removing them at night.

8. Give yourself an air bath when you air the house (if you have a place where you have privacy, that is). Open the windows, take off all your clothes and walk around, do your exercises, and let your skin breathe.

If your teeth, your sinuses, and your digestion are in good shape, your breath should be pleasant. If in doubt, drink a glass of orange juice, chew a piece of Clorets gum, or use a mouthwash before coming in contact with other people. Get a little spray that can be carried in your purse and used in restrooms or in private when you wish to freshen your breath.

You can make your own mouthwash. Just get a few chlorophyll tablets from the drug store, dissolve them in water in a jar, and use the solution for mouthwash. This can be used for underarm deodorizer too.

Feet First

Good feet are very important when you are older. Consistent care will keep them in shape. It is not necessary to spend money to have good-looking, comfortable feet.

Twice a week, I apply the lanolin-vaseline mix to my feet, put on some heavy knit slippers, and pad about in them while I'm doing my morning chores. Some people might prefer to use this at night with bedsocks.

After I've washed and set my hair and while I'm under the dryer, I soak my feet in a pan of warm water with a bit of laundry bleach and table salt added. Then I trim and smooth the nails, push back the cuticle with a blunt file, and put a fresh blade in my little razor and shave the callouses gently away. The bleach softens them so you can use a very gentle touch. I then scour the heels and bottoms of my feet with sandpaper. I glued some rough sandpaper to the ends of a large, empty spool for this purpose. If you prefer to spend three dollars or more for a foot-scraping tool, you can—it does the same thing as the sandpaper spool. Then I massage in the hand lotion–glycerin liquid. I don't care for colored polish on old-lady feet, so I don't use polish. But, if you wanted to, you could, using the paint brush to apply it and putting cotton between your toes. Every morning I use more of the lotion on my feet and legs and push the cuticle back.

You must wear shoes that really fit your feet, especially when walking. Shop around until you find a make of shoe that feels wonderful, and always buy this make of shoe. Letting shoes get run over and out of shape is bad for your feet. If you have shoe trees, use them; and have the heels of your shoes straightened whenever they need it.

Shoes should be shined every day or two. You do your own, of course, applying polish with an old toothbrush or a little sponge and polishing with a brush, a shoeshine cloth, or a piece of your old flannel nightie. If shoes get a little loose from age and wear, get some heel pads from the dime store and stick them in yourself. If they come unglued, use a bit of household cement to keep them in place permanently. If the inner linings of your shoes wear out, get some new ones, cut them to fit, and stick these in place yourself too. You don't need to pay a cobbler to do these simple things.

You can extend the life of your shoes by keeping them in good repair. Nothing makes one look so poverty-stricken and beat-down as shapeless, unpolished shoes with run-over heels. You should never be caught wearing this kind of shoe, certainly not around the house or even in the yard. Get some of the sturdy kind to wear in the yard and garden.

When you walk, do try to keep your toes pointing straight ahead. Many old people walk with their toes splaying outward and shuffle instead of lifting their feet. Whether they walk this way because they are old, or whether this ungainly walk makes them seem unsteady and awkward on their feet, I don't know.

I walked behind a woman for several blocks the other day. She had an unusually long, quick stride, and when I caught up with her at a red light, I couldn't believe it. She must have been eighty-five. Trim and straight as a stick, she walked like a woman of thirty in something of a hurry.

Shop for the kind of shoes that will enable you to lengthen your stride and step out when you walk. Fast walking is good for you and makes you look and feel young again—alert, alive, and glowing with health and vitality.

11.

Free Fun and How to Find It

Fun, after fifty, is doing what you want to do. If there is nothing you want to do, that's sad, and you must discover something. If you have work you enjoy, that comes under the heading of fun. Don't give it up until you have to. If you have work you don't enjoy, give it up as soon as possible and launch a second career that's more to your liking. I did this, and I have never enjoyed life so much—though I do not earn a great deal doing what I enjoy.

When you live frugally, as most of us must, there isn't much money for fun things, so you must find ways of enjoying yourself that cost nothing or very little.

What do you really enjoy? Fishing, bridge, golf, TV, reading, sewing, handwork, playing games, listening to music, visiting, walking, cooking, or traveling? Everyone's idea of fun is different, so make a list of things *you* enjoy and note how many of these things can be done for nearly nothing. The chances are, there will be a good many, now that you are older. Then start doing them. Do not sit and feel sorry

for yourself because you cannot afford some of the things
you used to enjoy.

Most of my fun costs nothing these days. In fact, many
things I enjoy, such as walking, gardening, canning, preserving, sewing, painting, fixing, designing and making things,
not only cost nothing but enable me to live very cheaply. I
also enjoy visiting and entertaining, going places, running
about, and reading—very inexpensive pleasures if you manage them properly.

I do miss the opera, plays, and symphony concerts, lectures, movies, eating out in expensive restaurants, and the
nightclub performances I used to enjoy in my more affluent
days, and I am glad that I had an opportunity to enjoy
them. That is probably why I do not mind living frugally
now. Now, I look for and find fun things that are available
in the community and that are free or almost so.

Free Community Entertainment

Every community of any size provides some free or almost
free entertainment. All one has to do is look for it and take
advantage of it. The daily paper usually informs one of the
many free things to be enjoyed: band concerts in the park;
organ recitals and choir performances at the local churches;
art shows; craft shows and fairs; book reviews; movies; and
an occasional lecture—things to do and see and go to that
cost nothing or almost nothing.

The Public Library

The free public library is a fascinating place for those of
us who are poor and like to read. We can go to the library
and read all the magazines and check out the books that we
always wanted to read but never had time for. Those of us
who are readers have it made. We find reading the best form
of entertainment there is, and also the cheapest.

One of my happiest days of the week is the day I spend
at the library reading the magazines, taking a few notes, and

selecting books to bring home. I can read such magazines as *National Geographic, The New Yorker, Vogue,* and *Saturday Review,* expensive magazines that I can no longer afford to subscribe to. I used to buy these magazines at the newsstand and read many paperbacks (a very expensive habit), but I no longer buy any books at all. I can get all the best sellers at the library by putting my name on a waiting list. When available, they are sent to me by mail. I can read all the classics I missed and reread those I loved, savoring them anew. Reading becomes one of life's greatest pleasures when one is old.

The library is a great source of information too. If there is anything at all you want to know about or want to learn to do, appropriate books and materials can be found in the public library. Most libraries have now expanded their services to include tapes, records, pictures, slides, exhibits, and programs. There is a complete and completely free education waiting for you at the public library, and now there is time to take advantage of all its pleasures.

In the summer, I take my lunch with me and picnic in the park with the squirrels. In the winter, I slip across the street and have lunch in the tearoom and, after an afternoon of magazine reading, walk home in the brisk near-dusk, carrying my treasures in my tote, having had hours of enjoyment for nothing.

I subscribe to *Time* magazine; the subscription comes out of my fun money because I enjoy reading it at leisure in the evening. It keeps one current and gives one something interesting to think and talk about. If you take advantage of special rates that are occasionally offered, it is not too expensive.

Inexpensive Classes

People who like to learn to do things in the company of others can take classes instead of learning from library books. Most classes can be had for under ten dollars if you shop around. There are adult education classes at the local high school, classes at the YWCA and the YMCA, continuing education classes for older people, classes at city recreation centers, and classes especially designed for senior citizens. I seldom pay more than ten dollars for a class, usually less, and I seldom take more than one class at a time, so my fun money stretches and I also get more out of the class. Since retirement, I have taken classes in crochet, macrame, woodworking, watercolor, ceramics, yoga, crewel embroidery, sewing, photography, bread making, aerobic dancing, and swimming, and I am presently looking around for inexpensive classes in music and art appreciation, world history, Spanish, and dancing. Eventually, I will find them.

One always meets interesting people in a class. Even if you don't make friends, you make acquaintances. You mingle pleasantly with other people, many of them younger than you. You often get a new perspective and a broadened outlook.

People Fun

People are important to those of us who are alone; therefore, use some of that precious fun money to get yourself in contact with other people. Join some groups, some clubs, or some organizations; go where people are. On ten dollars a month, you can't afford to pay dues and participate in a half dozen groups or organizations at one time, but you can join one or two a year, find the ones that give you the most pleasure, and continue with them, dropping the ones you don't particularly enjoy or that are composed of people with whom you have little in common. I join at least one new group or organization a year, as well as learn to do one completely new thing.

When I first came to the city, I joined the American Association of University Women and a group of retired businesswomen, but dropped them at the end of the year to join the American Association of Retired Persons; a golden years group at church, which has potluck dinner meetings and de-lightful programs once a month; and a travel club, which has monthly luncheon meetings and travel films at a local cafe-teria.

Later, I will join a Great Books discussion group that meets at the library, the League of Women Voters, and per-haps a volunteer group of women who teach reading to illiter-ate adults.

There are a few expenses besides dues connected with "be-longing." There is transportation to and from the meeting place—and eating. I walk to all the daytime happenings, and, when I can choose what I eat, I choose to eat lightly—for a dollar or a little more, keeping both my figure and my money. At night it is often necessary to take a taxi home and pay a fare, but this is the price one pays for the privilege of meeting people, some of whom might become friends. Some do become friends—and take you home.

Entertaining and Friends

Once you've met people, you can take the initiative for friendship. You can learn to entertain very simply but nicely. Experiment with a few inexpensive recipes that come out well before you invite people you've met to supper and a few pleasant hours of conversation or as a prelude to a play or some other entertainment that they're driving you to.

Occasionally—not very often—there will be money for a little theater play, a ballet, a concert, or an evening on the town. But there is always sightseeing and exploring and pok-ing about in the new and strange places of your community.

Sightseeing in Your Community

Once a week, I go look-shopping, ride the bus to a new shopping center (or an old one), and go in every store to browse and see what they have; when I need things I always know where to go to find them cheaply. I gather ideas for things to make and do and write about, talk with strangers, have a light lunch in a place that looks interesting, and find my way home again on foot, taking in some parts of the city I wouldn't otherwise see. This would be more fun, perhaps, if there were someone to share it, but few people like to walk and look as much or as long as I. So I look and walk alone, and my lovely day has cost me nothing but a one-way, half-price carfare and the price of a salad lunch.

The Men in Your Life—Or the Lack of Them

Occasionally you will meet a charming, attractive, older man who can afford to take you places you can't go on your own and offer you entertainment you can't have by yourself. But don't count on it. The proportion of older women to older men is great. The competition is terrific, and the percentages are against you.

Too, if an older man is sincerely charming, attractive, and sufficiently well-off to matter, he can find a younger woman, more attractive, more glamorous, and sexier than you—and the chances are he will. So, the possibility of finding a desirable escort is quite remote, and you should not lose any sleep over the fact that there are no men in your life at the moment—and probably won't ever be.

There may be some man no better off financially than you who would like a housekeeper, a companion, or a nurse for nothing. My feeling is that you should take a trip with him before you definitely decide to give up your freedom and start sharing permanently. You really don't know people at all until you have traveled with them. Plan to be gone for at least six weeks—and preferably for six months, if he can afford it.

If, at the end of that time, you are still compatible and/or enamored with one another, marriage may be in order. It may be, however, that after this little junket, you will decide that freedom is a beautiful thing and that you prefer him as a friend rather than a husband.

If you desire companionship or sex without any permanent involvement—and some older women do—be discreet. The young can live together openly without marriage, but it makes us older ones appear to be a bit trashy. But, with discretion, the best of both worlds can be yours.

12.

Gifts and Giving

Giving gifts to those you love becomes one of life's greatest pleasures as one grows old. There is no money to buy expensive, elaborate gifts, but instead of spending money, you have time to spend—and thought. Inexpensive gifts are often just as beautiful, perhaps even more appropriate, and many times more appreciated than those that cost much more.

I make everything I give, and my gifts cost very little. Or, I give what my friend calls a token gift, a tiny gadget or remembrance that costs not more than a dollar. My friend, whose income is very limited, has a large family, including a number of small grandchildren. She loathes shopping and never made anything in her life, so she simply sends a dollar bill in a birthday card at every birthday, and she makes a point of never missing. The gift is known as "Grandma's dollar" and is looked forward to as a sure thing.

To keep track of birthdays, anniversaries, and other occasions you want to remember, ask for the little free booklet at a card shop in which to list these occasions—or mark them on a big yearly calendar—so you can spend your gift money accordingly, plan what you are going to give in advance, and not have to rush out and buy something at the last moment. These hurried, last-minute gifts are almost always expensive and usually not very thoughtful.

I have another friend who simply announced when she retired that there would be no more gifts at all, and requested that no one give her anything either. She says this works out fine for her and simplifies her life considerably. She also eliminated all greeting cards, Christmas cards, and so on. Instead, she writes a little note on fold-over stationery, much less expensive than a card, and calls it Christmas.

Most of us will wish, not to eliminate giving entirely, but to cut down. Since I enjoy making and designing things for others and their houses, as well as for myself and my house, I start planning and making my Christmas gifts in January. By Thanksgiving, I have them finished, wrapped, and filed away in my gift-storage chest. Then I can relax and let myself enjoy the Christmas season without hassle or hurry.

Early and Inexpensive Preparation

The time to buy wrapping paper and ribbon is the week after Christmas, not the week before. The dime store will have paper and trimmings greatly reduced. Ribbon bows will be packaged at twenty for a dollar. Christmas cards and stationery are also usually marked down the day after Christmas.

I try to make everyone something they really want or need. By beginning early, I have time to listen, and when people I love express a need or desire for something, I make a mental note of it. I also encourage them to tell me frankly what they want and would like to have.

I very often try out the design or idea for myself first— this is why I budget "things for house and gifts" together. One Christmas, I made kitchen appliance covers for everyone, in colors that matched their kitchens, after I had made a set for myself. For a few dollars I had gifts that would have cost ten times that much had I bought them at the department store where I saw them.

Getting Ideas for Things to Make and Give

I always search the women's homemaking magazines for things to make and give. Sometimes I copy these ideas, more often I adapt and simplify them. I also look through the pattern books in fabric shops and department stores. Many of the magazines put out special magazines telling how to make and do things that are appropriate for giving. These special magazines may be examined before one buys. They are on sale at newsstands and in hobby, craft, and needlework sections of department stores.

When I was taking a course in macrame, everyone on my list got a macrame item. When I was taking a class in ceramics, everybody received a ceramic piece. When I was playing with papier mâché, I made everyone some painted bracelets. When I embroider or quilt or otherwise construct a cushion that someone admires, they may receive a similar one. It's much easier to make something the second time around.

If you don't like to make things, start early on your Christmas shopping, and store gifts as you purchase them. You'll find things on sale; you'll be able to get things with coupons and with Green Stamps; you'll be given gifts you can't use that someone on your list can.

The little mail-order catalogs that clutter our mailboxes very often have interesting little gadget-type gifts for a couple of dollars. If you don't make things, you may want to order some of these things and keep them on hand for giving.

Little Gifts

A tiny, thoughtful gift is often more appreciated than an expensive one that the recipient hasn't any use for. When you haven't much money to spend, strive to give these thoughtful little gifts. I have given a number of little odds and ends to a wealthy friend who travels extensively, to take on her travels. When I took a trip with her recently, she still had and was using every one of the things.

Miscellaneous Gifts

I keep in my gift box a dozen or so little miscellaneous gifts, most of them handmade from scraps, such as pot holders; hand towels; placemats; sachets; chocheted baby shoes, caps, and blocks; crocheted scarves; glasses cases; small macrame and ceramic pieces; and other odds and ends to be brought out and used whenever I need an unexpected gift for some special occasion. So I never have to rush out and buy anything.

Goodies as Gifts

I never bake fattening goodies for myself, but at Christmas time my friends get baked goodies in small containers, sweet remembrances instead of a card or gift. I save coffee cans and small shortening cans and make cookies, fruitcake, candied and stuffed fruit, and sugared nuts; I put in a sample of each after I've covered the can with paper and lined it with foil. I top the can with a ribbon bow pasted in place, and no further wrapping is required. There is only a taste of everything, but many of my older and shut-in friends who have no opportunity or inclination to bake anymore welcome this bit of homemade sweets.

You don't need to be a baker of note to give goodies. There are many good recipes for "no bake" sweets: a can of carmel corn; a jar of pickles or sweet relish or preserves; or a can of homemade holiday crunch makes a nice little goody gift. A friend always gives me a pint of her brandied peaches because she knows I enjoy them.

Gifts for Children

The children on my list usually get a stuffed toy or a garment of some kind. You can make a toy or a small garment for a dollar or two—or for nothing if you have scraps, and people who sew always seem to. I also buy scraps for a song at garage sales. Often one can buy a big bag of scraps for a dollar. Teenage granddaughters like very skimpy bikinis in summer and sleeveless crocheted tops in winter. Very often I can get these out of scraps too.

Give Services Instead of Things

Instead of giving things, you can give services. I have several young friends to whom I give baby sitting services for an evening while they go out. This is my wedding anniversary present to them.

I often perform some onerous task that a working mother never has time for. Even though she may have household help, these tasks never seem to get done. I take a sewing box home with me to sort and straighten, add a new tape measure, a wrist pincushion or small sewing supplies, and return the entire box with a big birthday bow and a gift tag. I have cleaned and refurbished innumerable closets for young friends and relatives; I use a pretty sheet to make shelf edgings, cover boxes and hangers, and make shoe bags, purse hangers, or whatever else is needed to organize and beautify their closets. This is a gift that always seems to be appreciated, as most people do not have time for this sort of thing.

I have inserted piles of loose photographs in albums and copied favorite recipes lying messily in drawers and filed them in a new recipe box; I have put slides in order. The amount I spend on these gifts is minimal, but the service is always appreciated, especially by working mothers, and these are gifts that an older person with time to spare can easily give. Naturally, one must know quite well the people for whom these services are performed. One could not be stirring about in the closet of a casual acquaintance, or putting her slides in order either.

Children, accompanied by a friend or two, can be taken to the zoo, to the swimming pool, or to the skating rink for a birthday treat; they can also come to your place and have birthday cake and ice cream. This is the type of afternoon that only a doting grandmother could possibly enjoy, and working mothers will love you.

Children want the expensive gadgets they see on TV, of course; but they also like homemade doll clothes and doll houses, their own pictures and stories made into a scrapbook, a handbound book about themselves written by Granny, or a photograph album filled with pictures of themselves from babyhood till now with some empty pages for later photographs.

Gift Wrapping

Gift wrapping has become an expensive addition to gift giving—the wrapping, card, and ribbon cost as much as the homemade gift, and the time and effort spent in wrapping a gift is a lost cause. Instead of simply wrapping your gifts, cover and decorate boxes to put them in as you complete the gifts. The recipient can find a use for the box as well as for the gift.

Making Gift Boxes

Beautiful gift boxes can be created for practically nothing. You probably have most of the necessary materials on hand.

Be on the lookout for boxes in appropriate dimensions with removable lids; such lids are essential. Shoe boxes, hat boxes, stocking boxes, stationery boxes, and strong suit boxes, if they are the right size, are perfect. I pick boxes out of other people's trash and swoop through the dime store early in the day when they are unpacking their merchandise.

The box can be covered with beautiful wrapping paper, wallpaper, shelf paper, or whatever you have on hand. The easiest way is to first measure and cut pieces to cover the sides of the box with a two-inch overlap all around. Spread out each piece and smear paste over all with a brush and apply the paper to the side of the box, overlapping the edges at top and bottom and ends.

Then, cut end pieces to the exact measurements with an overlap only at the top and bottom and paste in place. Cut a bottom piece to the exact measurements and paste to the bottom. You can line the inside of the box with crumpled tissue paper or foil. You can either use water mixed with wheat paste, which you buy at the wallpaper store, or you can make your own. It's cheaper, of course, to make your own. Mix ordinary flour to a smooth paste with a little cold water, add boiling water, and cook to the consistency of thick cream. Spread it on the paper with a paint brush or slosh it on with a rag.

The decorations make these boxes beautiful and special. Add a purchased ribbon bow, a handful of little Christmas bells, a tiny ceramic piece, a pair of yarn dolls, pompons or tassels made from leftover yarn, or cutouts from paper lace doilies or old Christmas cards. A roll of wallpaper will cover innumerable boxes, and wallpaper is the easiest to work with. Shelf paper and giftwrapping paper are more fragile but do nicely. The creases in a piece of used wrapping paper can be pressed out with a warm iron.

Inexpensive Conventional Wrapping

If you don't want to cover boxes, you can use inexpensive or free materials for ordinary wrapping. I sometimes use kitchen foil, pastel or deep-hued tissue paper, the want ad section of the newspaper, or a piece of burlap, on which I chainstitch simple decorations and then whipstitch the package shut with yarn or floss. I use sewing scraps for decorations—bits of lace, rickrack, tape, sequins, buttons, felt, artificial flowers, toothpicks, cereal, macaroni, dried seeds and pods, and straws. Yarn can be twisted into cord and used in place of ribbon. Strips of calico can be pinked with a pinking shears and used as ribbon for tying or to make bows.

Getting Ideas for Unusual Wrappings

At Christmastime, many magazines feature unusual and beautiful gift wrappings. I save these and adapt the ideas, using my inexpensive boxes, paper, and decorations.

Greeting Cards from Scraps

What about cards you send or give to friends, acquaintances, and relatives—Christmas cards, birthday cards, anniversary cards, get well cards, and bon voyage cards? They cost from fifteen cents to a dollar a card these days, and they can eat a hole in a dollar-a-day budget. But you can make your own for pennies apiece. One good way to keep yourself from ever feeling lonely or depressed is to have something interesting to do, something creative and fun, and making cards is one of these things.

Some homemade cards are beautiful works of art; usually they are created and constructed by arty people and require expensive and elaborate paper and other materials. You'll see these in books and magazines. Directions and patterns are included, and it is occasionally fun to try duplicating or creating similar cards, especially for Christmas.

However, these cards may be as expensive as the kind you buy, because you often have to buy special materials and paper. If you want to make gay and interesting little penny greetings, you use inexpensive materials you have on hand. I make up a dozen or more cards at a time so I always have one on hand when I need it.

Embroidered cards cost very little because they are made of scraps from the piece bag, odds and ends of leftover embroidery floss, homemade paste, and construction paper. All you buy is the construction paper. You can get a package of 9-by-12-inch construction paper in assorted colors from the dime store. Measure and cut a piece of paper in half crosswise, and then fold it to make a booklet 6 by 4½ inches.

I usually put my embroidery on a piece of eggshell colored

or natural burlap, cutting the burlap about 4½ by 3¼ inches and fringing it more or less evenly on all sides. Then I embroider "Love" or "Joy" or some such in chain stitch and decorate the surrounding area a bit with lazy daisy flowers, cross-stitch, or French knots worked here and there. Then I lightly paste the burlap to the card front.

A scrap of linenlike fabric, huck toweling, or similar material can be used. This lends itself to somewhat finer embroidery. I draw in a circle by tracing around a dime, then use different colors in outline stitch and French knots, completely filling in the center of the circle and extending it to the size I want. I paste the embroidered piece to the front of the card and frame it with another piece of paper cut the same size as the front with the center cut out. One Christmas, I embroidered Christmas cards by working satin-stitch candles, wreaths, bells, holly, and Christmas trees on pieces of real linen.

I like these embroidered cards because you don't need to trace or copy patterns—you can work freehand. For the more elaborate cards, you can pencil sketch the figure on the fabric. The more artistic you are, the more artistic the card. You can make them as elaborate or as simple as you wish.

To make an envelope to fit the card, use another piece of construction paper in a matching or contrasting color. You can also make an envelope from a piece of brown wrapping paper or white butcher paper. When you use this kind of paper, line the envelope with shelf paper or wallpaper cut from a wallpaper book or a piece of gift-wrapping paper. Put the card on a piece of wrapping paper and draw a diamond shape around it, so that the corners of the card reach almost to the sides of the diamond. The envelope should be a little bigger than the card so it will slip easily inside. Use a ruler to keep the lines straight. Fold the two end pieces in and then the bottom piece up over them, and paste in place. Cut the lining paper and insert.

13.

Travel on a Shoestring

Travel broadens our horizons, expands our interests, and gives us something to look forward to. That is one of the secrets of a happy and fulfilling old age—to always have something to look forward to in joyful anticipation; to look not back, but ahead. Travel fills the bill for many of us— we look forward with a great deal of pleasure to seeing new places, hobnobbing with new and different people, and talking with them and realizing our sameness.

Many of us never had time to travel when we were younger—we were busy making a living. We had family responsibilities, children to look after and to send to college. Travel was something that had to wait. Now, of course, we have time to travel. All we need is the money. It does take money to travel—*some* money—not too much if you know how and where to cut the corners.

How to Travel When You Are Alone and Timid

Old ladies who have not traveled very much and are timid about traveling alone should probably begin with a conducted tour; perhaps go on a conducted tour with a friend and stay in a twin-bedded room. It's cheaper that way. Otherwise, you pay extra for what is known as a single supplement.

It's well not to book a long tour with even your best friend unless you've first tried out the arrangement on a short tour. Even though you've known her, or him, for years, you don't really know people at all until you've traveled with them.

Lacking a friend, you can ask the tour company or travel agent to find a roommate for you and eliminate the single supplement fee. You may hit it off beautifully with the stranger the agency has selected for you. Some of my best friends are people that I first shared a room with on a trip—and it's nice to have friends in strategic areas across the continent or world.

This arrangement may not work out so well—you may despise each other on sight. This is the chance you take, but any civilized person should be able to put up with another, no matter how weird, for a week or two. You can ignore each other completely except at night, and think of the money you're saving!

Choose Your Tour Carefully

There are posh, expensive tours, and there are inexpensive ones. On the expensive tours, you stay at the more expensive hotels and eat a bit more—usually about the only difference —and the room you have may not be any better than one at a smaller, less expensive hotel down the street, into which the less expensive tours are booked. If you choose carefully —and you should comparison shop for tours, the way you shop for everything else—you can often see more for less.

Tours to avoid are those where all or most of the meals are furnished. This makes them more expensive, and nobody needs three square meals a day when traveling. On such fare, most of us will be square or well on the way when we return; and if you don't eat the meals you've already paid for in the package deal, you're wasting all kinds of money. To save both your money and your figure, book a tour where you buy your own meals.

Save on Food

For about $1.50 you can invest in a little immersion heater that you put in a cup to make your own morning coffee. Take with you a folding cup, a spoon, and some powered coffee in little paper envelopes. If you must have food, go out the night before and buy a roll and some fruit from the grocery. Or, pack some breakfast bars and some packages of instant breakfast.

I take Tang and tea in envelopes. Instead of buying a soft drink for a dollar when I come in from sightseeing, I have a glass of Tang or tea with free ice from the hotel's ice bin.

I order only a dinner salad and crackers for lunch, which costs a dollar or less at most lunch stops. In the evening, I often buy a carton of cottage cheese, a carton of yogurt, and some fruit and again eat in my room. This makes a good, high-potein meal, more nutritious than most meals you'd pay five dollars for in the hotel coffee shop. I take Lipton's instant soup in little flat packages, and I sometimes have only a cup or two of soup for dinner with some crackers that I've saved from lunch. I take a can opener and occasionally buy a little can of something—sardines, baked beans, or fruit that I can eat from the can with my spoon.

Eating this way gives me more time to sightsee. There's no waiting around for an hour or two every evening waiting to be served. The food and equipment will fold up flat and go into a little plastic bag in a suitcase. Occasionally I dress up and have dinner in some festive and fashionable place—I enjoy spending my food money this way, rather than having a mediocre meal every night.

Limit the Number of Photographs You Take

Another way to have a cheap trip is to limit the number of pictures you take and buy postcards, which cost from ten to fifteen cents apiece, instead. One can spend a fortune on film and developing, and photography is not the proper hobby for a poor old woman. Since I want the pictures for my scrapbook, I buy cards selectively—only those things I have actually seen. These cards are pictures of buildings, parks, and typical city and country scenes, better than I could take with my little Instamatic camera. I use the camera only for off-the-beaten path pictures—a chipmunk on the trail, a child leading a burro, or tea brewing in a sun jar. I allow myself only two rolls of film per trip, not enough to endanger my budget but enough to personalize the scrapbook I make upon my return.

These scrapbooks enable me to enjoy the same trip many times. They contain the postcards; my own photographs; pictures and descriptions cut from the brochures I've collected; notes I've taken; and the day-by-day journal I've kept. This is the way to get a lot of travel enjoyment out of a little travel money. I get out my books and look through them on cold and rainy Sunday afternoons that might otherwise be lonely, and I am immediately transported to some far and fascinating place where I have been, lost for hours in happy remembering.

Eliminate Taxis and Tips

Taking only one suitcase or backpack that you can carry yourself cuts down on taxi fares and tips to bell boys and others. A couple of three-block taxi rides with a tip or two at each end can shatter a ten-dollar bill. If all your clothes go together, all the clothes you need will fit into a small suitcase. When planning your wardrobe, plan it for travel so you won't have to buy a single new thing for the trip.

Take Everything You Need with You

Cosmetics, cigarettes, aspirin, film, shoe polish, and other odds and ends will cost much less at home than at the hotel drugstore, and you won't have to spend your sightseeing time doing mundane shopping. Buy deodorant, hair spray, and toothpaste in small sizes especially for travel and store them in your cosmetic kit so you are always ready to go.

Do Your Own Hair and Nails

In my more affluent days I always had my hair done and my nails manicured at the hotel beauty shop. With tips here and there, this can amount to eighteen or twenty dollars. Now, I go with my nails unpolished, and I take shampoo and a few rollers and clips with me. I wash my own hair under the shower, let it partially dry, put up the top in rollers and the back and sides in pin curls, and sleep on it. The next morning my hair is dry. It does not look quite as well, perhaps, but it will do, and it has cost me nothing. If you must have your hair and nails done, it's usually possible to find a cheaper place down the street from the hotel. Some people travel in wigs.

Don't Overtip

But don't be chintzy either. Old women have a reputation for either being chintzy or overtipping due to generosity or ignorance. If you ask for or require special services, you are expected to pay for them—and you should. Being old and poor and alone does not take you off the hook. In most restaurants, a tip of 15 percent is adequate. If the service is bad and the waiter impossible or discourteous, don't tip at all, but it's not his fault if the food is poor. The same is true of taxi drivers. If they get out of the cab and help with your luggage, tip them. If they sit there and pretend not to notice your bag, give them a token tip or nothing at all. Remember when taxi drivers used to get out just to open the door? They don't do this anymore—don't expect it.

On most tours tipping will be taken care of. If you don't know how much to tip in a strange city or a foreign country, ask the guide what is customary. A good guidebook will tell you about tipping, although these books can sometimes be a little out of date.

Be a Look-Shopper

Another way to save money is to be a look-shopper rather than an actual shopper. Many people spend hundreds of dollars buying things on trips, things for themselves and gifts for everyone they know. I'd much rather go on more trips. I usually buy one small thing to put on my around-the-world shelf or a charm for my bracelet for five dollars or less. This is the extent of my shopping. I can look-shop and admire for hours in order to find what I want. A friend buys a spoon for her spoon collection; another buys a thimble. These are nice, inexpensive things to collect.

Be Smart About Money

When you cross a border, know what the exchange is. The guidebook will tell you about the currency of a foreign country. Exchange your traveler's checks at a bank, if possible, not at the hotel, as the exchange is usually better at the bank. Don't get more money than you need. Take a fistful of dollar bills with you and go with a bit of currency from the countries in which you will be traveling if you can get it at your bank.

Travel on Your Own

If you are traveling in this country or another English-speaking country, or if you speak the language of a country even poorly or slightly, you can usually travel much cheaper on your own than you can on a tour. To enjoy traveling this way, however, you must have traveled enough to know your way around and how to maneuver.

I went to Santa Fe, New Mexico, recently and spent a week in the area. A travel agency had sent me a brochure describing an eight-day group tour that included all meals and a stay at an expensive lodge several miles from the center of the city. Instead, I went alone on the bus, had a wonderful time, did and saw everything that was listed in the brochure and a lot that wasn't. The cost of my trip was less than half the price of the tour with a single supplement.

The Cheapest Way to Travel

Bus travel is the cheapest kind of travel, and I find it fun. You see much more than if you go by plane. I never ride more than one night on the bus. The second night I stop over. The thing to do is to start your trip in the evening and ride the first night while you are not yet tired. If you go to the back of the bus, the chances are greater that you'll have a seat to yourself, much more restful than if you have to share. You can curl up, use your purse and sweater for a pillow, and spend a fairly restful night. You ride all the next day but get off at night and stop over, as you do on subsequent nights. Be sure your ticket is written this way. Much stopping over will run up the price of your trip, of course. For long distances, therefore, a plane may be almost as cheap, but you must figure the cost of getting to and from the airport, taxi fares, etc.

Bus station food is usually very bad, but many times there are other eating places close to the station that you can try. Or, take a bit of food with you—a buttered bun or some breakfast bars. Many people do.

Going by Plane

A good travel agent can be a big help with plane reservations and fares. Ask her to find you the most inexpensive flights. There are cheap flights without frills—charter flights and those you can book well in advance to save you all kinds of money. Take advantage of these. Sometimes agents can book you flights with stopovers that enable you to see much more for less. Discuss all the possibilities with the agent. You can save yourself the price of a meal by eating on the plane.

Book a 5:30 flight instead of a 3:30 one so you will be served dinner en route.

Going by Boat

If you want to go inexpensively on a cruise of any kind, you have to have a friend with you. A single cabin will usually cost you nearly twice what it would cost if you shared a cabin. You really can't afford not to share.

A freighter or cargo ship is much cheaper than a cruise ship, but it's difficult to book passage on a freighter, and there is a question of age limit. A travel agent who specializes in freighter trips can help you.

The Best and Cheapest Trips

Probably the best and cheapest trips for older women are those that you do partly on your own and partly by tour. The American Association of Retired Persons has tours for older people. The pace is slower and you are well looked after, but they are often rather expensive. But, some of their "extended vacation" packages are not at all expensive. In the winter of 1976 I spent six weeks on the Costa del Sol in Spain with them. Airfare from New York to Malaga, Spain, and return, plus six weeks' rent on a roomy apartment overlooking the Mediterranean, with single supplement, was only $700, a real bargain. The accommodations were not posh, but they were adequate. Food was comparatively cheap in Spain, as was local transportation. So were hotels if you studied the guidebook and knew where to go.

Once in Spain, the optional trips and excursions sponsored by the AARP were rather expensive, as always, but once there you could go out on your own if you were so inclined and were prepared with a smattering of Spanish.

While on a tour to Morocco, I met a marvelous woman who had the instincts of a homing pigeon and spoke quite good Spanish. She liked to travel the way I do—fast and on foot, taking advantage of Spain's excellent and cheap public transportation. We went on a series of very inexpensive junkets together and had some fascinating experiences, the kind you cannot possibly have on a conducted tour.

The AARP has extended vacations in other places, although Spain is one of their cheaper ones—you can stay as long as three months if you wish and can afford it. They also have extended vacations in Florida, Hawaii, Italy, Switzerland, Britain, France, Mexico, Morocco, and Canada. You will meet many interesting older people on these extended vacations, and the staff attempts to provide a variety of entertainment. In Spain there were dances, craft classes, musicals, dance classes, cooking classes, nightclub entertainment, bingo, and what have you, as well as free bus service into the center of town. You can obtain information about these extended vacations by asking for the AARP brochures.

A good, economy-minded travel agent—and you may have to look hard to find one—can help you plan and prepare similar trips, which I find cheaper and more interesting than a tour. I found such an agent who helped me plan my first post-retirement junket. I explored Hong Kong, Singapore, Bangkok, and Kathmandu, taking some tours after I arrived in each city. Then I went on an already-arranged seventy-day bus tour from Kathmandu to London through Afghanistan, Pakistan, India, Iran, Turkey, Greece, and on to London. I would not have enjoyed traveling alone through some of these countries.

Once in London and on my own again, I rented what is known as a bed–sitting room and settled down to enjoy this fascinating city; I went on some one-, two-, and three-day tours to Ireland, Scotland, Wales, and places on the Continent with rest stops in between at my London flat.

I booked these tours with London travel agents and went with British people who know how to travel cheaply, stopping at hotels with bathrooms down the hall at about half the price of a room with a bath, which most Americans insist upon. A friend joined me later, and we rented a horse-drawn caravan and toured a piece of Ireland, driving the horse from place to place and cooking and sleeping in the caravan.

There is no reason why an old woman cannot travel by herself and do it cheaply. If you keep yourself in good shape and good health, and if you keep yourself agile with exercise, there is no reason why you cannot enjoy travel when you are old, old.

I met a ninety-three-year-old woman traveling with a group from Australia when I was in Canada. She did not go on all the side trips that required a lot of walking, and sometimes she stayed in the bus and took in the view from the window, but she was enjoying herself thoroughly. It was her first trip outside Australia. She'd won a lottery of some kind. Most of us won't be lucky enough to win a lottery, but we can save our money to travel on.

Traveling for Nothing

There are ways to travel for nothing. This involves some work, of course, and the work is usually more suitable for a younger person. However, there are ways that older people, if agile and well preserved, can travel for nothing also. I know one woman who goes along several times a year as a companion of a very wealthy old woman who likes to travel. All her expenses are paid. She does have to make arrangements as they go along, and to take care of details, but the work is not difficult and the lady she accompanies not unpleasant.

I know another, a former housewife, who manages to "go on holiday" three or four months every winter and several months in the summer. She stays at home only in the spring and fall. She is older, but she is still an excellent cook and competent housekeeper, loves children and old people, and has a pleasant personality. In the past years she has been to Phoenix, Juneau, La Jolla, Miami, Atlanta, San Francisco, and Palm Springs.

She puts an ad in the city's paper in the "Situations

Wanted" section, requesting work as a live-in domestic. Sometimes she also contacts an employment agency in the city where she wants to go. The response to her ad is usually quite good. Letters and references are exchanged, and arrangements such as salary, duties, and time off are arrived at by mail. Her salary is usually sufficient to pay her travel expenses there and back and to sightsee on her days off.

Once or twice, she tells me, the job was not as outlined. Someone wanted her to scrub down the walls of a fourteen-room house and keep it spotless and shining, as well as do the shopping, cooking, and laundry for a family of eight. She simply contacted an agency in the city, got another job she could handle comfortably, and left. She had no trouble because domestics are hard to find.

Most people she has worked for are extremely considerate, she says, and do not expect an almost-seventy-year-old woman to scrub ceilings. She states frankly in her letters what she can and cannot do, the hours she will work, and the salary she must have—enough to pay her travel expenses. She has excellent references from her former employers which she photocopies and encloses. Since her salary requirements are not exorbitant, her duties are usually comparatively light also. Sometimes they involve only house-sitting while her employers travel. Sometimes they involve being a companion-housekeeper for an elderly person, the easiest job of all, she says. She seems to enjoy this getting away for nothing so much, I'm going to try it myself one of these days.

If you are a fairly rugged, vagabond-type traveler and not too fussy about where you stay and the kind of accommodations you have, write to the Council on International Education Exchange, 777 UN Plaza, New York, N.Y., 11007 for the book, *Where to Stay: U.S.A.* It costs about $3.50 and outlines low-cost accommodations across the country, state by state and city by city, including local tourist information and a myriad of information that this type of traveler will want to have. You may be able to make your own reservations by using this book. By going on the bus you will see a lot for a little—and have some fascinating experiences. In my opinion, the people who insist on going first class miss a lot. First class is not as much *fun* as tourist.

Your anecdotes are more interesting too. You can tell about the birds building a nest in your hotel room in Khajuraho, or the monkeys going through your suitcase in Jaipur. First-class travelers do not spin yarns like these.

Most foreigners are very nice to old ladies traveling alone or in pairs. If you are a pleasant old lady, not too fastidious or fussy, you will have an absolute ball abroad on the extra you save from your Social Security.

14.

The Mature Figure –
How to Get Rid
of It for Nothing

One morning I woke up and discovered I looked exactly like a penguin. I had what is known as a "mature figure." Translated bluntly, this means fat and lumpy and thick through the middle. Many older women are plagued with a mature figure, usually the result of too many calories and lack of exercise rather than age.

After an initial and firm resolve, it is posible to get rid of a mature figure if you attack it slowly and sensibly, the only way for most of us. Once rid of it, a mere shadow of your former self, you will feel a freer, healthier, happier person. Hidden beneath the rolls and lumps and bulges, there is still a shapely and attractive you.

In my opinion, fat is ugly on anyone past the age of two. I have never been able, as some of my friends do, to console myself that I'm less wrinkled when I'm fat. It's true, but I would rather be wrinkled. Neither have I ever been able to convince myself that I remained fat though eating like a bird. Sometimes I did eat lightly, but at other times I ate like a rhinoceros.

The truth of the matter is that we older ones have to consistently eat much less than we did when younger to maintain the same weight and figure. The smaller we are, the less we can eat and not gain. A big, broad-boned woman can eat twice as much as a little five foot one and still stay shapely. We little people have a tough time. It takes only a few calories to maintain us, and the other calories turn immediately to fat.

Plagued with a weight problem for years, I had reduced innumerable times to a point of being only mildly plump and occasionally downright thin, and then promptly gained back everything I'd painfully dieted off. For years I had clothes in three sizes.

Now that I had plenty of time to work on myself and no reasons at all to eat compulsively, I decided to throw out my diets—I collected diets the way some people collect stamps—and plan my own eating regimen that I could live with for the rest of my life. I believe that every fat person who wants to reduce and stay reduced must do the same. You must do your own thing, taking into consideration the way *you* like to live and eat, the foods *you* like and can have, and eliminating forever those you can't.

Following for a few weeks or months a diet planned by someone else may reduce you temporarily, but it does no permanent good, because the day you go off *their* diet and return to your former eating habits, which made you fat in the first place, all the pounds lost, usually plus a few more, are going to creep right back on.

Once a person has those fat cells, they are going to fill right up again. This is a sad fact of life for us fatties. Once a fatty, always a fatty. You may be a thin fatty, but basically you are still a fatty. If you relax, even for a day or two, those excess pounds are right back on you where they used to be.

Yes, I liked the goody-fattening stuff. My favorite recipes began: "Take a half cup of butter and a cup of brown sugar. . . ." I was able to resist these fattening goodies much of the time, but not all the time, which is why my weight went up and down like a yo-yo. Some people, poor dears, are not ever able to resist the fattening stuff and eat themselves past the point of no return so that losing the weight they should seems hopeless; consequently, they keep right on stuffing themselves into greater obesity. For these people reducing under a doctor's care might be a solution—or some other drastic measure such as going to a fat farm, where the amount and kind of food is monitored by someone else.

I have a wealthy friend who goes at least once a year to a fat farm and loses thirty to forty pounds. It costs her about $3,000—very *expensive* lard which she gains back in the next four or five months because the near-fasting diet used at this particular place does nothing to change her basic eating habits or her way of thinking about herself and about food.

Reducing is big, big business. Every year fat people spend millons of dollars on pills, belts, saunas, weightwatching groups, exercise machines, and classes and books telling them how to reduce. But it is not necessary to spend a single cent to reduce. In fact, by learning to eat lightly of the simple, healthful foods that keep you thin and healthy, you can actually save money rather than spend it.

One has only to look at the supermarket carts laden with all the expensive things that make people fat—prepared mixes and sugared cereals, white bread and sticky buns, beautiful steaks and roasts and chops marbled with fat, baked goodies and candy, nuts and whipping cream, chocolate, coconut, marshmallows, potato chips, and butter. These are the expensive foods.

Almost every woman's magazine you pick up has an article on a new way to lose weight, some new diet or other, but the same magazine contains page after page of recipes for luscious, calorie-laden goodies guaranteed to put back the pounds just dieted off. These recipes should be marked like cigarette advertising: "Dangerous to your health and appearance."

Obesity is unhealthful—everyone knows this and doctors

constantly admonish the overweight to reduce. Obesity leads
to diabetes, heart trouble, high blood pressure, and all the
other ills that the elderly are heir to. Recently I visited an exercise class for arthritics—all but two of the participants were
from 20 to 100 pounds overweight.

Thin people tend to live longer, more healthfully, and more
happily than the fat ones. When one is older, even ten pounds
of fat scattered here and there is too much. It's a strain to
carry it around. Think how heavy that ten-pound sack of
groceries becomes when you carry it home from the store.
That extra ten pounds of fat you carry around every day is
just as heavy—and definitely less attractive.

Anyone who wants to get rid of a mature figure can do it.
But first, you have to decide for yourself two things: How
much eating is over-eating for me? and when do I overeat
and why? Then you are ready to go about changing your
eating behavior and, to a certain extent, your way of life.

Your weight-losing regime won't be the same as mine, because you must plan your own diet around the things you
like to eat and the way you like to live; your doctor's orders,
if any; and your own particular health problems. But, all
reducing regimes have certain things in common.

Aside from my weight problem, I have no health problems.
I'm never sick, seldom tired, have few aches and pains, and
have sufficient energy to do anything I want to do. For years
I've eaten homemade yogurt and bread, whole grain cereals,
brewer's yeast, bran, wheat germ, liver, fish, cottage cheese,
skim milk powder, alfalfa sprouts, crisp raw vegetables,
fresh fruits, nuts and seeds—along with the occasional goody
stuff. Diets planned by other people don't ordinarily include
many of these foods which I think contribute to my good
health and which I really like.

There are foods I resolved to give up *forever*. They are not
good for you, even if you are not fat, and if you are fat, they
are fatal. They are:

1. Luscious, fattening, baked desserts made with white sugar and white flour. (These are things every fat lady must give up permanently if she wants to stay thin permanently.)
2. All prepared mixes and convenience foods, because they put all kinds of things in them you shouldn't have.
3. All junk food such as potato chips, candy, doughnuts, cookies, sticky buns, pizza, soft drinks of any kind, popcorn, alcohol, salted nuts, and crackers.
4. All visible animal fat. This includes cream, butter, ice cream, cream cheese, whole milk, and expensive meat with a lot of hidden fat.
5. Fried foods. This includes browning meat in butter or oil prior to cooking.
6. Sweet gelatin salads and desserts made with whipped cream, cream cheese, nuts, marshmallows, coconut, and so on.
7. Macaroni, spaghetti, noodles, and white rice, which contain practically nothing but starch, but not brown rice or beans, which contain some protein.
8. Refined, processed, store-bought cereals.
9. White bread and rolls.
10. Excessively salty foods.

By cutting out all these forbidden foods, schooling myself to eat *only one* helping at meal time and eliminating *all* between-meal eating—I don't permit myself so much as a piece of celery between meals—I lost about a pound a week.

If you have more than twenty pounds to lose, I recommend taking a whole year to lose it, because it takes almost that long to learn to control your eating behavior and change your eating patterns and habits. At the end of the year, you will have learned how to stay permanently thin.

My overeating was largely habit and largely psychological. You may find that yours is too. We eat not only because we are hungry but because we are bored, frustrated, tired, or concerned about some trivial problem, and because the forbidden foods are there. If they're not there, you can't eat them. Stuffing ourselves makes us feel better momentarily. Sweets are both a reward and a solace.

It is not easy to break the pattern of the years, but it can be done. Be prepared to suffer a bit. But gradually, the desire for large quantities of food will lessen and eating the goodies will become less important than looking good, and you will suffer only a little and only momentarily.

There were certain things I did to get myself started on my new regime, tricks of cooking that made it easier to cut calories without actually counting them, and behavior modification techniques that made it possible for me to permanently change my eating behavior. Perhaps some of these will help you to plan your new way of eating and help you to stick with it:

Get Interested in Something Else

Get your mind off food. This is a very important step for most of us. I got very interested in writing my first novel, which turned out to be a disaster, but when I had finished it, I was thin.

I know a woman who was planning a trip to Europe, and she knitted herself thin. She started knitting and crocheting herself a new wardrobe in a size ten, and when she finished, she could wear it. She dieted, walked, knitted, and crocheted for eight months. I asked her how she managed to stay with her diet for that long—she never had before—and she said she thought about her trip and looking great in her new clothes instead of cooking, her former hobby—and she *did* look great in her new clothes.

If you like to knit or do handwork or crafts of any kind, try this. I find that if I get at my nonfrustrating crochet or embroidery, it does take my mind off food. Sewing helps me too. Making a beautiful garment in a size eight takes me through two or three days of near-fasting.

Don't Buy Forbidden Foods

For six months don't buy a single forbidden food on your list. Give your company your new-regimen food too. Chances are, they won't even notice because it's not all that drastic. Thinness starts at the grocery store. Here, the person who lives alone has it all over the one who is cooking for a family, although the family would probably be better off if mamma fed them her diet food too. Obesity is the number one health problem in America today. Even the young ones are getting fat on snacks and fats and sweets and junk food, and middle-aged husbands keel over with heart attacks and strokes caused by too much rich, sugary, buttery, fat-laden food.

Don't Tempt Yourself

Don't keep anything in the house that tempts you to nibble or eat compulsively. The will power of fat people is fragile. If you have anything forbidden on hand, give it away or hide it. Put it on top of the cupboard so you will have to get a chair and a yardstick to reach it. No one eats compulsively on raw cabbage and celery sticks, which can be safely kept in the refrigerator.

Get Rid of Fattening Recipes

Go through your recipe file and throw out every favorite fattening goody you are never going to make again—all the baked desserts containing quantities of sugar, the gelatin salads laden with forbidden ingredients, and those that begin by browning meat in added fat or oil. If you can't bring yourself to throw out these recipes, hide them from yourself. I avoid recipes and recipe books. Just reading them sends me on an eating kick.

You won't need to pass up all the goodies, however, be-

cause you can very often substitute low-calorie for high-calorie ingredients. Personally, I dislike the taste of sugar substitutes and never use them. I'd rather have a raw apple than a
piece of apple pie made with artificial sweetener and imitation
crust. It's certainly easier too. But there are other substitutions
I use frequently. The end results are not as good, perhaps,
but they will do.

When a recipe calls for sour cream, I use homemade low-
fat yogurt.

When a recipe calls for whipping cream or whipped topping, I can occasionally use whipped skim milk powder.

When a recipe calls for cream cheese, I whip low-fat cottage cheese in the blender.

Instead of sautéing vegetables in butter, I put *one* teaspoon
of margarine in a nonstick skillet, add a bouillon cube and a
bit of water, and stir until the vegetables are limp. The bouillon cube provides all the salt I find necessary.

I make imitation cream to eat on cereal by mixing equal
parts of skim milk powder and ice water and putting it in
the refrigerator. This tastes sweet so you need very little or
no sugar on cereal.

Cut Way Down on Sugar and Oil

But, don't cut them out entirely. I found that eliminating
sugar completely made me feel deprived. Feeling deprived is
what makes one go into the kitchen and eat the whole pie.
So I do season with a little sugar. I have a baked apple occasionally or a cup of custard, and I buy the sweetened canned
fruit to mix with yogurt, but I keep the portions of these
sugared foods small.

Small amounts of fat and oil are also necessary for health.
They keep you from feeling hungry and they force water out
of the system. A complete absence of fat and oil makes for
dry skin and an all-gone feeling, which makes it difficult
to stay on a low-calorie regimen for any length of time.

Lose Weight Slowly

Don't plan to lose rapidly on any regimen. Be content with small, constant losses each week. I weigh myself every day, and if I have gained from the day before, I give myself an *X,* which means cut those portions *down.* I keep track of my weight on a little monthly chart. The first of the month I expect to be at least three pounds lighter than the previous month when I'm reducing, and I expect to be exactly the same when I'm not.

I found it takes at least a year to permanently change your eating habits and to get your appetite under complete control so you'll never get fat again. If you have fifty pounds to lose, lose a pound a week. If you must lose a hundred pounds, aim for two pounds a week. The fatter you are, the faster you tend to lose, so it is not hopeless even if you must lose a hundred pounds. It should take a year or a little more.

Eat Regularly

Have three tiny, tasty, nicely served meals each and every day. Sit down at the same place at the same time with place-mat, silver, and a fresh napkin, and eat slowly, enjoying every morsel. This was very difficult for me to do because, like many fat people, I was a fast eater and I often ate "on the run."

If you skip a meal to hurry the losing process, you'll be doubly hungry at the next one and eat three times too much. Also, no standing in the kitchen and eating cottage cheese out of the carton, as many live-alone people do. You eat much more than you think that way.

Since night eating was a problem with me—I stay up late and get really hungry at night—I had a late breakfast, a three-o'clock lunch, and an eight-o'clock dinner. I had a skim milk-shake at anywhere from ten to twelve o'clock. This is not the best way to do it, but it worked for me, and that is the idea behind planning your own regimen—you can do anything that works for you.

No Snacking

No snacking is permitted on my regimen. When I start snacking, I don't stop. Some people will have better luck eating five or six tiny meals a day, but this didn't work for me. Once I get started eating, I eat non-stop all day. The only exception is the milkshake every night as a special treat. This milkshake enables me to stay on my regimen without undue suffering, makes me feel comfortably full and cozy, and I have it when I need it—at night.

Eat Slowly

Linger longer over every meal. Eat slowly. Have salads and crunchy foods which take a long time to eat. Have a grapefruit juice cocktail before eating; finish each meal with a leisurely cup of herb tea or a demitasse of black coffee. If you eat for an hour, at the end of that time you'll feel that you've had enough.

Don't Measure Food

Don't try to count calories or carbohydrate or protein grams or anything else; you are not on a diet, just eating sensibly and lightly. But, it behooves one to know which are low-calorie and which are high-calorie foods and the calorie content of some high- and low-calorie foods you will be using. For instance, in every tablespoon of fat and oil of any kind—butter, margarine, mayonnaise, etc.—there are 100 calories. If you put two tablespoons of oil and vinegar dressing on a low-calorie salad, you've added 175 calories.

A tablespoon of sugar is about forty calories. To burn these calories, you will have to walk a fast mile. It's easier not to use the sugar.

Celery is very low-calorie food; so are mushrooms, raw cabbage, spinach, and tomato juice. Some people call these foods deficit-calorie food—you supposedly use more calories eating and digesting them than they provide. However, some of these low-calorie, bulky foods have a high salt content, and if you have a water-retention problem, the scales won't show any weight loss. This is always discouraging.

You should also know the foods that are high in protein in relation to their calorie content. These are good foods for most fatties—cottage cheese, skim milk powder, liver, brewer's yeast, fish, and fowl.

Eat Only One Serving

Put one serving of everything on your pretty little plate—and that's it. Serve yourself in the kitchen, then put the remains right into the refrigerator so you won't be tempted to have another spoonful—or another portion when cleaning up. It's already in the refrigerator, cooling and congealed.

Eat Simply

Don't have too much variety or too many dishes at any one meal. Have a salad with yogurt or creamy cottage cheese dressing. Have meat or a plant protein, a piece of whole grain bread or melba toast spread with cottage cheese, and a light dessert. Or, have a hearty portion of a vegetable-protein casserole, some raw vegetables on the side, a whole wheat muffin, and fresh fruit for dessert.

Use margarine as a spread for bread or toast very rarely; use low-fat cottage cheese mixed with yogurt instead.

Eat a large, thinning salad with a piece of crunchy toast or bread *first*. This fills you up and makes you want less of the higher-calorie food. A friend reduced by doing only two things: starting every meal with a big, crisp vegetable salad, and ending with a piece of fresh fruit, her only dessert for a year.

Appetite Killers

Half an hour before every meal drink a glass of water with a bit of unsweetened grapefruit juice added. When hungry between meals, drink this also. Learn to drink water instead of eating between meals. Water is good for the dieter; it flushes out the residue of the burned fat.

Eat a Balanced Diet

Plan balanced meals—some protein which the body requires to maintain itself; a *little* fat and oil which keeps you from getting hungry and tends to rid tissues of excess water; something crisp and crunchy which takes a long time to eat, some fiber and roughage; and something very mildly sweet such as fresh fruit or fruited yogurt to put a period to your meal and keep you happy until the next one.

Salt

Omit it entirely if you can. If you can't, use it sparingly.

Learn About Quantities

If you are not losing on your regimen, get a little scales and weigh servings for a few days to see how much a four-ounce serving of meat or six-ounce serving of salad or vegetable really is. You may be eating more than you think.

Exercise

Walk; swim; dance; hurry about instead of poking along when doing your housework; stand instead of sitting. Exercise won't reduce you unless you spend hours at it, but it does burn up a few excess calories, it makes you feel fit and toned, and, yes, it keeps you from getting hungry.

Avoid Scoffers

Avoid people who want you to stay fat and encourage you in all kinds of subtle ways to do so. One of their favorite ploys is to tell you your face looks drawn and haggard. This may be true, but when you get reduced and stay that way for six months, your face will fill out somewhat and you will look wonderful.

Or, they will tell you kindly that you aren't fat, you look

great. Either they're lying or they can't see the lumps under your clothes. You know they're there though, and you hate them. Or, they will tell you *how* you should lose weight, about some new diet or other that's sure to take off fifteen to twenty pounds a month. Pay no attention to this kind of talk and stay with your own regimen.

Avoid Situations That Require Eating

I dropped out of a couple of clubs that had dinner meetings and served fattening food. When I eat at a restaurant, I order a dinner salad, nothing else. When I'm invited to a friend's house, I eat as lightly as possible but make no mention of my diet or food preferences, even though it means going off my regimen. Chronic dieters are a great bore.

Don't Start Out Hungry

Never go hungry to the grocery store, out to eat, or for dinner with friends. Fill yourself with vegetable sticks, bran soup, and water with a little grapefruit juice added before you leave the house. I go to the grocery right after breakfast or lunch, make a shopping list, and get only the things on my list, so I'm not tempted to do any extra looking or impulse buying.

Be Sensible

Use discretion when planning one-dish meals and casseroles. Instead of having tuna and noodles, make it tuna and spinach; instead of chicken and dumplings, make a chicken and chopped broccoli casserole. Don't cut carbohydrates out, cut them down.

Get Support

Get a friend or relative or an interested someone to support you in your program. Ask her to weigh you every week at the same time and on the same scales. This often makes the difference between staying on your regimen and not staying on it. Such help will take the place of the support and advice given in the weight-losing groups for which you pay a fat fee.

I have a fat friend in for a salad supper every Thursday evening. (I should say a formerly fat friend.) We both lost weight on our personally planned programs. She could eat twice as much as I and she lost more rapidly and twice as much, but we both reached our goal. Most of us need that extra bit of support that another person can give.

Learn to Be a Little Hungry

If you would be permanently thin, get used to hunger; school yourself to hunger. Some people must work harder and suffer more to be thin than others. Those who are small-framed, those who were fat children and consequently have a larger number of fat cells, and those who are older and less active than younger people of the same size and build will have a more difficult time losing weight and keeping it off. It is unrealistic for those people to expect to lose weight and keep it off without ever being hungry. Rather than giving in to hunger pangs and nibbling at the first sign of discomfort, it is necessary to school yourself to withstand hunger. It is necessary to train yourself to be hungry and not eat.

It took me years to accept the fact that I had to be hungry to get and maintain a decent figure. I kept trying to find a diet that would permit me to lose weight painlessly and without hunger. For some of us there is no such diet. Once you accept that fact, you can start training yourself to be hungry.

I do this by being *very* hungry one day out of every week. One day a week I have only large glasses of very diluted grapefruit juice for breakfast and for lunch, and an orange juice-banana skim milkshake for dinner. No matter how hungry I get, I don't eat. I assume I can stand anything for one day. As I work at conquering hunger, being hungry bothers me less and less. Since I am very hungry just one day a week, the mild hunger that I experience on my lessened food regimen does not bother me unduly.

On my near-fasting day I take a nap in the afternoon and go to bed early. Sleep eases hunger, and if you are lucky, you will be a pound lighter the next morning. But don't fool yourself you've lost a pound of fat. You haven't. You've lost water and salt and you will gain back most of that lost pound when you resume eating.

Play for Keeps

Always think of your regimen as forever. Don't look forward to the day you can go off it and resume your old way of eating. If it made you fat in the first place, it will make you fat again. Likewise, your new regimen will keep you thin for the rest of your life. Don't look forward to holidays or trips or visits as times when you can go on an eating binge.

Learn to distinguish between real hunger and the desire to eat that is compulsive. If a subconscious craving is making you want to eat, try to figure out what it is and, if possible, let yourself have it. There are other ways of compensating for loneliness, boredom, and frustration besides eating. When you discover what they are, you will have conquered your compulsive eating.

You must keep yourself "psyched up" and stay motivated. Getting myself "psyched up" to lose weight has never been difficult for me, but staying that way is another matter, and it is absolutely necessary to stay that way. One sees fat people who have become thin and look great, and after a couple of years or the next time you see them, they are fat again. They didn't or couldn't stay "psyched up."

Meditation helps some people. It helped me. Sitting in a chair with my eyes closed and visualizing myself thin helped. I visualized myself standing on the scales and weighing 105 pounds. Crazy? A little. But so is overeating. Playing games with myself helped—engaging in little fantasies.

But one must be able to separate fact and fantasy. You should not believe that being thinner is going to drastically change your life. It won't, especially if you are pushing seventy. We'll be the same people with the same problems and the same personalities—we'll just be thinner and feel better about ourselves; more in command of ourselves, at least in command of our appetites; and look better and get around better—reward enough. Believing that life is going to be suddenly beautiful when you are thin is a big mistake, because, when you *are* thin and life goes on much the same as it always did, disillusionment may set in. This kind of thinking can easily trigger overeating again.

Instead, think health and longevity. Think of all the overweight people you know who are ailing and decrepit and spending all their spare time and money running to the doctor. Think of all the thin ones who are dashing off to Europe and Hawaii, spending the winter in Florida, learning new skills and polishing up their old ones, giving of themselves, and having a gay time. With which group do you wish to identify?

If you want to get thin and stay thin, you must *change* your thinking about food and about yourself. Don't think of the luscious piece of banana cake, or an apple pie oozing cinnamon and sugar, or a rib roast smothered in rich brown gravy, or the French pastry in the restaurant window as a reward or as something to be desired. Think of them as dangerous and detrimental to your health, and not as tasty as they look.

Think of *good* food, food that is good for you—a heaped plate of crispy, colorful vegetables piled around a dish of onion-flecked yogurt dip; a mound of creamy cottage cheese ringed with fresh, ripe fruit; the bright green of plain-cooked broccoli spears; the deep orange of carrot coins seasoned with a bit of grated onion and a bouillon cube. Eating the things that are bad for you is such a fleeting pleasure—a moment in your mouth and the rest of your life around your middle. It is no longer worth it. When you can think about food in this way, you can bid good-bye to the mature figure. Good-bye penguin.

Once you get used to light and simple eating, you won't crave quantities of rich, fattening food, overly salted and seasoned and sweetened. The less you eat of the rich, fattening gooey stuff, the better off you are, even if you are no longer a fat fatty. A thin fatty can become a fat fatty in a very short time, and that is the image you must have of yourself if you are to stay shapely: a thin fatty. You must always think of yourself as a fatty who is momentarily thin. The fat fatty is only an apple pie, a few hearty family dinners, and a couple of martinis away.

You Don't Need to Hurry

The greatest stumbling block to losing weight is expecting to lose rapidly—and becoming discouraged when you don't. Very often the discouragement will trigger a compulsive eating binge. When you plan to lose only a pound or two a week, this give you time to train your appetite and to eliminate forever the desire to overeat, which made you fat.

Most people, including me, would like to lose at least twenty pounds a month, the way the advertisements in the cheaper publications maintain is possible. You take a small multiple-vitamin pill, a piece of special gum or candy, exercise with a stretching or rolling gadget for only fifteen minutes a day, and presto, it's gone! Or, you put on a sauna suit or wrap a piece of elastic around your middle and lose twenty-eight pounds and fourteen inches (or some equally ridiculous amount) in a month or two.

That's just not possible when you analyze it, and these wishful-thinking advertisements help to keep a great many people fat. We fat people tend to look and hope for a way to reduce painlessly, and for most of us there is no painless way.

Each pound of fat represents 3,500 calories. A person who is only twenty pounds overweight has 70,000 excess calories clinging to him, or shall we say her. If that person maintains weight on 1,500 calories a day—and many older, not overly active women do—and she eats 1,000 calories a day for a week, she has a deficit of only 500 calories a day or 3,500 calories in a whole week—one pound of fat.

If she cuts her calories to 500 calories a day—and she is going to get very hungry on 500 calories a day and probably won't stay with it very long—but if she sticks with it for a week, she has a deficit of 1,000 calories a day or 7,000 in a week—and it is possible to lose two pounds of fat.

When food intake is cut drastically and suddenly, the scales may show for a few days or even a few weeks a weight loss of from one to four pounds a day. But that isn't fat—it couldn't be—it's water. The digestive tract is being emptied of its water due to the drastically lessened intake of food and salt, and this rate of loss will not continue after the first few days or weeks. It's arithmetically impossible.

People who manage to stay on a crash diet for ten days very often lose ten pounds—three pounds of fat, perhaps, and seven pounds of water. When they resume their normal eating, they gain back the seven pounds of water, probably within the next week or two. Some fat people who have a great deal of water stored in their tissues along with the fat will lose faster than those who do not have stores of water.

I have a very fat friend who visited me last year and insisted she wanted to join me in what she called my spartan regimen. The scales showed an amazing loss of fourteen pounds in just one week. She was delighted and thought she'd found the way at last to rapid reducing. When she returned home, she stuck with it for another week or two and lost only three pounds, so she gave up and went back to her own way of eating—or overeating. Her thinking was askew—she anticipated losing rapidly, and she had not embraced the regimen as a permanent thing.

Those who are known as the "beautiful people"—the wealthy, the successful, and the famous—are very seldom fat.

It is the middle-class middle-aged poor who so often let their figures go to pot. True, the wealthy have the money to spend to help them maintain their figures with massages, saunas, surgery, and visits to health farms and exercising salons, but we poor little people can keep our figures, too, and for nothing.

In fact, it costs less to eat ourselve thin than to eat ourselves into obesity, because small portions of the simple, healthful food cost less than quantities of the rich, fattening kind. In this respect, we can easily emulate the rich. We, too, can get and keep a shapely shape.

If the mature figure doesn't bother you and your doctor has given up on your weight problem, you may simply wish to let well enough alone and enjoy your three square meals a day with desserts and snacks in between. Three square meals a day will almost invariably make an older person square. We don't need that much food anymore. Everyone makes a choice, and it is up to each individual to decide how important to her eating is—whether eating is more important than a good figure.

15.

Dieting on a Dollar a Day

It's possible to diet on a dollar a day or less, because food intake is drastically curtailed and because low-calorie foods, if selected with discretion, are usually cheaper than high-calorie foods.

When you plan your own diet, you can include the low-calorie foods *you* enjoy. I think these foods contribute to the good health of an older person, and I plan my diet around them—yogurt, homemade with skim milk powder; alfalfa sprouts; skim milk powder milkshakes; cottage cheese; liver; bran; brewer's yeast; wheat germ; tomato, grapefruit, and lemon juice; lots of crisp, crunchy raw vegetables; fresh and canned fruit; canned sardines, mackerel, and tuna; eggs, a chicken now and then; lean ground beef; wheat; brown rice; beans; and bread made from soya, whole wheat, rye, and un-bleached flours.

I use not more than ½ pound of sugar and ½ pound of margarine a month. If I can find unsweetened canned fruit or fruit canned in light syrup, I buy it; if not, I use the sweetened kind and use it sparingly. I buy low-fat cottage cheese and the store brand of skim milk powder in the twenty-quart size.

Some of my food I buy at the health food store along with vitamins A, B, C, D, and E, which do not come out of my food budget. Perhaps the vitamins are not really necessary, but just to be on the safe side, I take them anyway.

To make the homemade yogurt, you need a carton of the plain yogurt bought from the health food store to use as a starter. The yogurt from the grocery is often pasteurized to kill the bacteria so it will keep, and it won't start more yogurt. I make salad dressing and vegetable dip from this yogurt; I also use it in recipes that call for sour cream, mix it with cottage cheese as a spread for bread and toast, and eat it for dessert mixed with fruit.

To grow alfalfa sprouts you need a package of alfalfa seeds from the health food store. Be sure to get them there because the seeds elsewhere are very often treated with a poisonous substance to promote their growth in soil.

I buy milled bran—the outside of the wheat berry—from the health food store. This is the cereal fiber that was so highly recommended some time ago by several physicians in their books. They maintain that the lack of sufficient fiber and roughage in the diet leads to all kinds of serious complications as we get older. This bran has no sweetener or additives, and it costs about sixty cents a pound. I eat this as cereal, put it in soup, and use it for making bran muffins and bran bread.

I buy brewer's yeast which I mix with tomato juice. The yeast I use comes in a can and is called "Super Yeast Plus, Formula 300." It is more than three dollars a pound, but it is high in protein, contains all the B vitamins and the following minerals: calcium, phosphorus, iron, copper, iodine, magnesium, potassium, zinc, manganese, and sodium. It has only forty-six calories per tablespoon.

I also buy from the health food store soya flour, which I use for making bread. It is high in protein but has to be used in combination with wheat flour. In place of cocoa, I use carob powder. It's supposedly better for you than cocoa or chocolate, and it makes a delicious milkshake and is much cheaper than cocoa or chocolate.

Wheat berries can be bought at the health food store, but they cost more than sixty cents a pound. I get wheat as it comes from the combine for nothing. The chaff has to be washed away, and then the berries are cooked in water, as is rice. The wheat is good tasting and good for you; it is very high in fiber, and contains not only the bran but the wheat germ and oil of the wheat berry. It's comparatively high in protein. I use it as a cereal, in salads, and as a vegetable.

Company is no problem on my regimen. Most of my friends watch their weight—or they should—and they do not want or need great quantities of rich, fattening food. It is no kindness to stuff one's company with unhealthful foods. Low-calorie foods look as beautiful as the fattening kind and taste just as good. In the summer I serve a supper salad with melba toast and a delicious hot bread in a basket. Later, I split and toast the hot bread.

The following list includes some of my favorite and less expensive foods. These are the foods that enable me to successfully diet on a dollar a day or less:

Homemade Yogurt

In a bowl mix 1½ cups of skim milk powder with 3 cups of warm water and two heaping tablespoons of the bought yogurt, fill the cups that come with the yogurt maker, cover them and set them on the plugged-in yogurt maker, and let set for six or seven hours. You need an electric yogurt maker which holds the milk at the correct temperature. (Some people can make it without a yogurt maker, holding the milk at the correct temperature in hot water.)

When the mixture is set, put the covered cups in the refrigerator. Use two tablespoons of this yogurt for a starter the next time you make it. It will make six or seven batches, but then you will need a fresh starter from the health food store. This homemade yogurt does not have quite the same texture or taste as bought yogurt, but it is much cheaper and I like it just as well. Some people think that stirring a small can of evaporated milk into each batch improves the flavor and texture. This, of course, makes it a bit more expensive and a bit more fattening.

Yogurt Salad Dressing or Vegetable Dip

This is a creamy, low-calorie dressing that's inexpensive and good. Scoop several cups of homemade yogurt (one-half the batch) into a square of porous material and let the whey drip out. Don't discard the whey. Put it in a jar of skim milk powder mixed with water and let it set in a warm place. If you catch it just right, it makes a delicious imitation buttermilk for drinking. Put it in the refrigerator and use this when a recipe calls for sour milk or buttermilk.

When the whey has dripped out of the yogurt, scrape it into a bowl and stir in two teaspoons of oil, two teaspoons of canned lemon juice, and a teaspoon of Hidden Valley salad dressing mix.

Onion Dip

Instead of Hidden Valley mix, add a little Lipton's onion soup mix. Stir the mix around a bit before adding it so you get some of the onion and some of the seasonings. Eat with crisp, raw vegetables.

Cottage Cheese Dressing

Low-fat cottage cheese makes the base for another low-calorie salad dressing. Take an eight-ounce carton of the cottage cheese, add three tablespoons of vinegar and a bit of water, and blend in the blender until creamy and smooth. Pour out and add seasonings to your taste. A bit of bleu cheese added to the dressing makes it special. Crumble up as much of the cheese as you can afford and stir it in. If you prefer the dressing smooth, put the bleu cheese in the blender. Though cottage cheese is not cheap, it is a good protein buy, calorie-wise.

Cottage Cheese–Yogurt Spread

Take ½ cup yogurt, blend it in the blender, add a small carton of low-fat cottage cheese, and blend until creamy and spreadable. This makes a low-fat, high-protein spread for bread and toast.

Protein Dessert

Put ½ cup cottage cheese in a sherbet dish and top like a sundae with yogurt mixed with canned fruit and juice. This has become one of my favorite desserts.

Skim Milk Shake

Put a cup of orange juice in the blender, add ⅓ cup skim milk powder and ½ banana, sliced. Add six ice cubes, one at a time, and continue blending until liquefied. This makes a tall glass of thick creamy shake which can be eaten with a spoon. This shake enables me to stay on my dieting regime— it satisfies my hunger better than anything else.

Milk Shakes Variations

Use ½ cup prune juice, two prunes, and ½ cup water. Or, add some frozen grape juice concentrate to the ice water or, use ½ cup of unsweetened shredded pineapple. Or, use a scoop of cranberry sauce, frozen raspberries, or cherry pie filling. Or, make an imitation chocolate shake from carob powder. Add to the skim milk in the blender a teaspoon of honey and a rounded teaspoon of carob powder and blend.

Or, omit the carob powder, and substitute maple, vanilla, or butter pecan flavoring, and toss in a few sunflower seeds and a tablespoon of soya flour.

Imitation Whipped Cream

Measure into a bowl ½ cup ice water, add ½ cup skim milk powder, and put in the refrigerator along with the beater. Let it get very cold before whipping. Add a teaspoon vanilla and a bit of sugar, to taste. This can be used in many recipes in place of whipped cream or the frozen whipped topping.

Imitation Cream for Cereal

Stir, don't whip the above. Keep in refrigerator and use on cereal. This tastes sweet and you'll want little or no sugar.

Imitation Chocolate Pudding

After whipping the skim milk powder, add vanilla, a little sugar (preferably powdered), and carob powder to taste and continue beating. Small grandchildren will probably like this pudding, and it can be made in a moment.

Variations on the Pudding

Instead of water, use orange juice, add two teaspoons of Tang or a little more to taste, and continue beating. Garnish with a bit of shredded, toasted coconut when serving to company.

Soya Protein Bread

This bread adds inexpensive protein to the dieter's diet. It makes very hard, crunchy melba toast. The recipe makes one loaf—double it for two—it can be frozen until needed for toast.

Put a package of yeast, ¼ cup warm water, and 1 teaspoon sugar in a bowl and let set until the yeast starts working.

Then measure into the sifter 2¼ cups unbleached flour,

¾ cup soya flour, 1 tablespoon sugar, and ½ teaspoon salt.

Mix ¼ cup skim milk powder with ¾ cup warm water, add two eggs, beaten, and 2 tablespoons melted margarine. Add the yeast mixture to this. Sift part of the dry ingredients into this and beat with beater. Stir in the rest of the flour with a spoon. Turn out on a floured board and knead until the dough feels elastic and springy. It may be necessary to add a bit more flour to keep the dough from sticking.

Put in an oiled bowl in the oven, cover, and let rise until doubled in bulk, which usually takes about 1½ hours. The oven is a good place to let bread rise; turn on the oven for thirty seconds, turn it off, and put the bread in.

When the dough is doubled in bulk, punch down, and then let it rise again. Then, shape it into a loaf and put it in a greased pan. Again, turn on the oven for thirty seconds and let the loaf rise until doubled in bulk. Heat oven to 350 degrees and bake for thirty-five to forty minutes. Remove from oven, cool slightly, and remove from pan.

To make crunchy melba toast, slice the loaf thinly, and toast it in a 300-degree oven for thirty minutes or until it is a beautiful shade of brown. To make garlic melba, melt a bit of margarine in a pan, add powdered garlic, and brush each slice of toast with a little of this, using a pastry brush.

Wheat

Wheat provides more roughage and fiber than almost any other food; and, when you are dieting, a lot of fiber and roughage is filling. Wash the wheat berries well to float off chaff by putting water in a kettle, then pouring off the water a number of times. (If you use the expensive health store wheat, this won't be necessary.) Cover the berries with water, bring them to a boil, and let them soak overnight. Again, bring them to a boil and cook until the water has boiled away and the berries are tender but not pasty. Watch carefully the last ten minutes or so. If overcooked, you will have wheat paste in the bottom of the pan. Store these berries in the refrigerator and use them for cereal, in salad, and as a vegetable. For cold cereal, put wheat berries in a bowl, slice half a banana over the top, and add imitation cream and sugar to taste. To use wheat as a vegetable, put a teaspoon of margarine in a small pan, add wheat berries and a whisper of garlic salt, and heat. To use wheat in a salad, toss in the wheat berries, grated carrots, a cut green onion, and some cut celery and mix with dressing thinned with a bit of yogurt. Serve on lettuce.

Hot Cracked Wheat Cereal

Wash berries as above. Cover them with hot water, put in a blender and blend until the wheat is cracked. Then pour the mixture into a pan and cook, stirring frequently until it thickens and the wheat is soft—from twenty to thirty minutes. Eat with imitation cream or a dot of margarine.

Perpetual Prunes, Uncooked and Unsweetened

Put a package of pitted prunes in a jar and pour boiling water over them. Let them·sit in the refrigerator for a day or two. The juice will thicken and taste sweet, and the prunes will soften. As I use the juice, I add more water. Thus, I have juice until the prunes are gone.

Reducer's Liver

Wash and devein sliced liver. Roll in instant onion flakes or cut up an onion very fine and roll the liver in the onion. Put the slices in a glass baking dish. Dissolve a bouillon cube in a bit of hot water and spoon half of it over the liver. The cube seasons and salts it sufficiently. Cook for twenty minutes in a 300-degree oven. Turn the liver, and spoon the rest of the bouillon water over it; and bake for another twenty minutes. Wrap leftover slices in foil, and reheat in the foil. Or grind it with bread crumbs, an onion, and a hard-boiled egg, add a mustardy dressing, and use it as a spread on toast.

Alfalfa Sprouts

Put two rounded teaspoons of seeds in a jar with warm water to soak overnight. The next morning fasten a square of double cheesecloth over the top of the jar with a rubber band and pour off the water. Shake the seeds around in the jar and put under the sink. Night and morning pour fresh water into the jar through the cheesecloth, rinse the seeds, and pour off the water. By the third or fourth day the sprouts will be ready for use. If the jar is put on a window sill in the light, they will green up.

To make an egg-mustard dressing for the sprouts, stir up in a pan an egg, 2 tablespoons vinegar, ¼ teaspoon mustard, a pinch of paprika, and a pinch of garlic salt. Cook until thick. Stir in a bit of oil and thin to your liking.

To make a sauerkraut and sprouts salad, open a can of sauerkraut, drain it well, and rinse a portion to remove as much salt as possible. Mix the kraut and the sprouts and toss them together with a tiny bit of oil and vinegar dressing and some caraway seeds.

Stuffed Mushrooms

Wash and clean mushrooms, remove the stems, and save them. Put the mushroom caps in cold salt water for a few minutes, and then stuff with blended cottage cheese and yo-gurt mixture seasoned with Hidden Valley salad dressing mix. (The original recipe calls for cream cheese.) The mushrooms are also expensive.

Chef's Salad

Tear up greens, shred carrots, and cut up peppers, celery, cucumbers, and green onions. Mix the salad with yogurt dress-ing and spoon it onto a lettuce-lined plate. Top with cauli-flower buds, tomatoes, sliced pickled beets, carrot ribbons, green pepper rings, cucumber slices, or whatever else you have. In the center of each plate lay a sardine and a hard-boiled egg, halved. Pass some separate dressings.

Fruit Salad for Two

Cut up a large orange, a big apple, and a banana, and mix them with a can of drained unsweetened pineapple chunks. Toss them with dressing thinned with a bit of pineapple juice. Line a plate with lettuce. Put a mound of cottage cheese or yogurt in the center, and arrange the fruit salad around this. Sprinkle with sunflower seeds for crunch.

Tomato Aspic Mold for Five or Six

In a bowl put a cup of cold tomato juice and sprinkle four packages of unflavored gelatin on top. Then heat six cups of tomato juice to boiling and in it dissolve two bouillon cubes. Pour this mixture over the gelatin and stir until it is dissolved. Let it cool in the refrigerator. When slightly thickened, add some cut up celery and green onion for crunch, and pour it into an oiled mold with a hollow center. When cold and set, unmold on a large plate. Fill the center with shredded raw carrots. Put lettuce or greens around the edge of the mold, arrange stuffed eggs around the aspic, and garnish with parsley, cucumber slices, or green pepper rings. Instead of the eggs you can use cauliflower or broccoli florets.

Winter Fare for Company

In the wintertime, I serve a big puffy omelet topped with cheese with a tossed salad lightly dressed with oil and vinegar and a loaf of hot, fresh-baked bread. Or, I have a chicken breast rolled in milk and seasoned protein crumbs before baking in the oven, a small fresh fruit salad, and either broccoli spears with lemon butter or carrot coins cooked in bouillon, seasoned with grated onion.

I usually have fruit desserts for company—a beautiful raw apple with a piece of cheese; sliced oranges sprinkled with a bit of cinnamon and sugar; streusel pears; a brandied peach topped with a spoon of ice cream; or a honey-glazed apple baked and split and topped with a hint of ice cream with some of the apple juice poured over. (A spoon of ice cream is permitted on company desserts when you have schooled yourself to leaving the rest of it in the freezer until the next time you have company.)

Eating Alone

When I'm alone, I have cereal, fruit, and milk for breakfast; a soup or salad lunch with toast and brewer's yeast stirred into tomato juice; and a light dinner with salad, a meat or protein dish, a slice of crunchy toast, and fruit or yogurt for dessert. I try to keep dinner light and long, crisp and crunchy, nicely arranged and pretty on the plate. In the late evening I have a skim milk shake.

This kind of eating is quick and easy—you don't spend much time in the kitchen preparing things and cleaning up— no grease on the stove and no mess in the oven from pies dripping juice and roasts spattering.

Short and Quickie Diets

If you have slipped off your regimen and want to knock off four or five recently-put-on pounds in a hurry, there are some three-day quickies that will do it.

If the scale suddenly shows a weight gain of four or five pounds, that isn't all fat; it's part water—that's why you can lose it in three or four days. It is possible, of course, to gain a pound of real fat in a day if you eat 3,500 excess calories, but you would have to overeat grossly and compulsively.

If you want to try these diets—and try them only if you can stand to be very hungry for a short period of time—here are the ones that work best for me.

Diet 1

Lemon water and diluted grapefruit juice for breakfast, plus a large bowl of clear vegetable soup three times a day, or a small bowl five times a day. (Cook carrots, celery, cabbage, peppers, onions, spinach with a bouillon cube, add a can of tomatoes. Make a lot of juice.)

Diet 2

Lemon water and diluted juice for breakfast. Milk shakes for lunch and dinner. (To these shakes you can add a tablespoon of bran and a tablespoon of soya flour for extra protein and roughage if you prefer.)

Diet 3

Chicken and liver diet. In the three days you can have one small oven-roasted chicken and one pound of liver prepared without any fat. (Don't eat it all the first day, of course.) Drink plenty of water. If you are one of those people who have trouble with carbohydrates, this may be for you.

Diet 4

Diluted grapefruit or orange juice for breakfast, plus not more than 1 cup of low-fat cottage cheese, ½ cup yogurt, and ⅓ can unsweetened pineapple or other unsweetened fruit daily. In addition, you can have as much uncooked or cooked low-carbohydrate vegetables as you want at meal-time—celery, cabbage, spinach, cucumbers, mushrooms, etc., with nothing added but a minimum of seasoning. (You can stuff the mushrooms with the cheese and yogurt and eat a whole plateful. You can have a whole package of spinach seasoned with lemon juice topped with a bit of yogurt. You can have a protein sundae—mix the yogurt with the fruit and pour over cottage cheese.)

Diet 5

The one-day fast. For one day, drink water with a little lemon, grapefruit, or orange juice added. In the evening have an orange juice-banana skim milk shake. (Or you can have the shake any time you need it most.)

In some of these quickie diets, quantities are limited, which accounts for their effectiveness. If you kept your food intake down to eight ounces or less, per day, you could probably eat peanut butter and jam and still lose weight. It is well to take a vitamin and mineral supplement when trying these quickie diets, because they are certainly not balanced, and they should not be followed for more than three days at a time. Most of them are very inexpensive—they make good end-of-the-month fare when the grocery money is running low. I don't recommend crash dieting, but occasionally I do it— *for not more than three days at a time.*

16.

Shaping Up at Seventy

Don't let anyone tell you that it's too late to do anything about your figure. It isn't. Naturally, one does not look like a magazine model at seventy, but it's possible, with healthful diet, appropriate exercise, and meticulous grooming, to improve one's appearance to the point where you will not be embarrassed at a family pool party—or even on a public beach.

Though I had reduced to an acceptable weight, I was still lumpy and shapeless with loose skin hanging. This is a very good reason why you should never let yourself get fat in the first place. Old skin has lost some of its elasticity and does not go in when you do. However, it can be coaxed back into some semblance of shape with appropriate exercise, massage, and lubrication.

If you stay with your eating regimen and step up your exercise program, the chances are that in six months or so a lot of the loathsome lumps will have disappeared. When the body adjusts to its new weight, it tends to shift some of the lumps around to other places and tighten in. Don't leave it all to chance though. The shaping process can be helped along with daily exercise and massage, the more the better.

One has to be realistic about the shaping business. Innate body build has a lot to do with the shape we're in. Some people are naturally cut on long, slender lines, and some of us are pear-shaped or square. But, being realistic is no reason for us pear-shaped ones to stuff ourselves on apple tarts for lunch, as many of us seem prone to do.

Excess fat is unsightly and unhealthful on any build. If you have fat showing beneath the skin, you are too fat, no matter what the height-weight tables tell you. Don't pay any attention to them or to what anyone else tells you either. Look at yourself without clothes in a full-length mirror. If the sight makes you shudder, plan an exercise program that you can and will do. Exercise is like dieting—you have to work out your own program. Only you know what you can bring yourself to do. A program planned by someone else soon becomes so boring you give up and don't do anything at all.

You don't need to go to a health club or an exercise class and spend a lot of money to exercise under supervision, although this tends to keep you at it while you're paying your money. But you *can* do it yourself—for nothing. You don't need to spend money for gadgets or machines or ropes or pulleys or belts or sauna suits either, as some of the magazine advertisements would have you believe. Time is all you need, time and the determination to get started. You feel so much better when you exercise regularly that you may decide it's really worth the effort and keep going.

How long it takes you to shape up depends on how bad you are when you start. Shaping up doesn't do any good, of course, unless you plan to stay in shape, and that means exercising and eating properly from now on. It takes as much exercise and will power to stay in shape as it does to get there, sometimes even more. But, if you are gutsy enough to stay with an exercise program and an eating regime that keeps you slim and limbered and lovely, you'll be the envy of your friends and acquaintances.

Walking is excellent exercise—fast walking, not strolling. Walking is probably the best exercise there is for old people, and it's something almost all of us can do.

Riding a bicycle, either real or stationary, is good if you have a place to ride it and a place to keep it. Jumping rope is excellent if you start out with just a few jumps a day and work up slowly—and if the jar doesn't hurt you anyplace. Running in place is good; aerobic dancing is another excellent exercise. The thing for old people to remember is not to do anything that hurts and to start all strenuous exercise very slowly.

Swimming is great exercise for smoothing out bulges and firming muscles and skin, and it doesn't make you stiff and sore. Instead, it tends to take the stiffness *out* of old joints and muscles. If you don't swim, consider learning. If you are able to get to and into a pool, you can learn to swim. I can now swim a half mile with quite a bit of huffing and puffing, and, after two years of instruction, I am only in the intermediate group at the YWCA. At this stage of the game, the level of performance is not all that important. We tend to do the things we enjoy, and since I enjoy both swimming and walking, I do them rather regularly. Aside from walking and swimming, I do stretch-and-bend exercises especially designed for lazy, older ladies. Many of these exercises are not strenuous enough to slim, but, if done regularly, they limber joints and stir up circulation and make you feel like a new and younger woman. If you start gradually, they do not make you stiff and sore. Then, if you concentrate on the spots that need it, they do seem to improve posture and trim flab.

I particularly wanted to get my shoulders up and back and my stomach in and to take the flab off my upper arms and the lumps off my legs. These are old-woman ugly spots; these figure flaws are common among middle-aged and older women. Look around you at the flabby arms, protruding stomachs, humped backs and slumped shoulders. These are not so much the results of age as of indifference, carelessness, laziness, and disuse. But, if you have let yourself go to pot because of lack of exercise, you can put yourself back together again with it.

Fast, strenuous exercises that hurt when you're doing them and for days afterward are not for us. These gentle-type exercises, with a few exceptions, are designed for older people. They start at the top of your head and go down to your feet and gently stretch and stir up everything in between. They can be done as many times as you feel like doing them or until boredom sets in. They can be done all at once or in two or three ten-to-fifteen-minute periods during the day or evening. You can do all of them or pick two or three in each set that please you. You can wear whatever you have on, although you will probably prefer to wear something loose.

Don't strain to do the ones you can't do; do what you comfortably can. For instance, if you can't bend over and touch your fingers to the floor without bending your knees, lean over as far as you can and bend your knees a bit.

Start at the Top of Your Head

Put your fingers on your head and move the scalp back and forth, around and around. Move the skin, not your fingers. Marvelous if your hair is getting thin on top, and whose isn't? Move every bit of scalp and then brush your hair vigorously for a few minutes, brushing it up and away from your scalp until your head feels tingly.

Face

Open your eyes and mouth as wide as possible. Make a huge face. Then squeeze both eyes and mouth shut as tight as possible.

Say the vowels *a, e, i, o, u* aloud, opening the mouth very wide and exaggerating the movements that make the sounds until you feel your mouth, jaws, neck, and even your nose working.

Neck

Nod your head slowly back and forth as far as it will go. The back motion is good for the chin line. Breath deeply in or out with every movement.

Turn your head from side to side as far as you can, slowly, with closed eyes, so you don't become dizzy.

Try to touch your ear to your shoulder, keeping your shoulders straight and letting your neck do all the work.

Shoulders

Raise your shoulders, then let them drop.

Bring your shoulders forward as far as possible, then push them back as far as possible.

Make circles with your shoulders: up, down, forward, and back.

Stand up, throw your head back, push your shoulders back vigorously by using your arms with your elbows bent to force them back.

Stand in a doorway, grasp the woodwork, and lean forward on your toes, keeping your body straight, until you feel a definite pull in your shoulders and arms. Then, pull yourself back to an upright position in the doorway. This is good for slouched shoulders and upper arms.

Swing each arm around and around rapidly, rotating your shoulders as you swing. Swing both clockwise and counter-clockwise.

Clasp both hands behind you with your fingers laced. Roll your elbows inward as vigorously as possible. This straightens the shoulders, thrusts the chest forward and up, and is good for the dowager's hump. Occasionally lean forward from the waist and let your clasped hands go high.

Hands and Fingers

Open and close your hands to make tight fists.

Spread your fingers as far as possible and wiggle your fingers.

Double your fingers down until the tips rest on the pads, at the top of your palm. Raise one finger at a time, keeping the other fingers in position or raise them all at once if you can't raise them singly at first.

Raise your arms in the air and shake them vigorously. Bring them down to your knees still shaking vigorously.

Rotate your hands from wrists both clockwise and counterclockwise, letting the fingers lead.

Arms

Letting your hands lead, rotate your arms at the elbows, moving them both clockwise and counterclockwise.

Extend your hands outward and shake your arms vigorously, shaking up the flab.

Stand about two and one-half feet from a wall. Put your hands on the wall. Now, lean forward on your toes, keeping your body straight, and touch your chin to the wall while resisting your body weight strenuously with your arms. Push your body back to position by straightening your arms.

Extend your arms to the sides, tighten your hands into fists, and bring them up toward your ears, trying to make big muscles the way your little grandsons do when showing off their prowess.

With your arms extended straight over your head, let your hands drop backwards down to your shoulders, feeling the pull in upper arms.

If you have a door top you can reach, hang on to it for a few seconds, letting your arms hold your whole weight.

Bosom

Extend your arms outward to the sides and make circles six to twelve inches in diameter with your hands.

Raise your arms to shoulder height, then raise them above your head; now lower them to face level in front of you, and then raise above head again.

Waist

Stand and extend your arms sideways, then twist from side to side, swinging your arms to give yourself greater momentum.

Stand, curve one arm over your head and bend sideways until your other hand touches your knee and creeps down your leg as far as you can go.

Bend at the waist and lean down, letting your hands flop, then straighten up and bend back as far as you comfortably can.

Extend your arms to the sides; then, with hands held high, stretch up as high as possible; then bend down and touch your hands to the floor without bending your knees.

Abdomen, Stomach

With your hands on your knees, sway your back as much as possible; let your stomach hang down; then slowly curve back up, with your hands still on your knees, pull your stomach in and up, and hold it.

From the same position, take a deep breath, blow it *all* out and suck your stomach in and up; hold it as long as possible.

From the same position, take a deep breath and blow it out, then alternately pull your stomach in and push it out as rapidly as possible.

Get down on your hands and knees. Arch your back like an angry cat and hold your stomach in, then sway back with your buttocks pushed up and let stomach hang down. Alternate back and forth between these positions.

Buttocks

Stand and tense your buttocks to lift, then relax. Repeat.

Hips and Thighs

Stand with your feet about twelve inches apart. Swing your left hand up in the air, and with your right hand reach down to touch the floor in front of your left foot. You should feel a pull in your hip and thigh. Then swing your right hand up in the air and reach down with your left hand to touch the floor in front of your right foot.

Pretend you are a striptease dancer, and move your hips, thighs, and waist in imitation; push your hips from side to side and from front to back, moving your arms, shoulders, and legs at the same time.

Stand with your left hand resting against a wall, keeping your body straight. Then raise your right leg up and back until you feel a pull on the left hip. Do the same with the left leg.

Stand with your feet apart as if you were going to do the splits. Bend your left knee, lean your weight to the left, straighten your right leg, and feel the pull on your inner thigh. Now, bend your right knee and stretch your left thigh.

Shake each leg vigorously.

Balance yourself with your left hand on a wall or chair back. Swing your right leg up and grasp your right ankle with your right hand, then lean forward and thrust your right thigh backward, still holding the ankle. This may hurt a bit at first.

Sit forward in a chair, grasp the seat with your hand, double up your legs, and raise your knees to chin level, then straighten your legs in the air and let them drop slowly.

Taking the same position, point your toes and raise your knees to your chin.

Stand and squat down slightly, keeping your feet flat on the floor, then bounce until you feel a pull in your legs.

Lean down and tense and relax your knees until you see the flesh move.

Stand with your feet about six inches apart and with your toes pointing in slightly. Raise yourself up and down on your toes until the muscles in your calves are tired.

Take hold of a chair back and swing one leg back and forth from your hip. Then swing the other leg after changing hands on the chair back.

Legs

Those with heavy legs might benefit from these leg exercises which you can do as you lie in bed. Exercising with your legs in the air is beneficial for many older women whose tissues tend to hold water and whose ankles swell.

Circle both legs together from the ankles, then from the knees; do both clockwise and counterclockwise.

Circle one leg from the hip, then the other, alternating.

Do a scissors kick with your legs.

Do a bicycle motion with your legs.

Kick your legs back and forth as in a flutter kick while swimming.

Slap your legs together vigorously, front to back, then slap the sides together.

Bend your legs at the knees, slap your calves to your thighs with kicks.

Lie in knees-to-chest position. Flex your knees toward your chest and shoulders. With one open hand on your left knee, press it as far as you can toward your left shoulder. Then press your right knee toward your right shoulder. Press hard, but do not jerk.

Massage—take your hands and dig into your lumpy flesh—squeeze and knead. As you lose weight, lumps become soft and you can pick them up in your hands. This kind of massage seems to be effective then. You don't need to pay someone to give you a massage; you can do it yourself.

I know a delightful eighty-year-old woman who keeps her own little house shining and spotless and in perfect repair, has a beatuiful yard and garden, and gets all her exercise that way. Wiry and thin, she is up early every morning working outside in her yard and garden—mowing, planting, raking, weeding, watering, picking, hoeing, stooping, and bending. She has no need for any other exercise program, as this work keeps her strong and agile. Most eighty-year-olds would find her work impossible, but she can still do it because she never stopped.

Most of us were not that clever. We stopped using our bodies and abused them with excesses. We ate too much and sat too much, and we got fat and tired. Now we are too old and feeble to do the things we did years ago. But, the body is resilient. It can be helped back to life and health and even beauty if we are willing to make the effort.

17.

Making a Little Extra

People of any age who are still on their feet and who still have their faculties can get a paying job and earn a little extra money—if they aren't too fussy about what they do.

Many retired people would like to work a bit and make the extra money they need to live more comfortably. Apart from the money, work tends to keep us with it, keeps us mentally and physically alert, and gets us out of the house and among people. Working also often enhances our self-esteem by fostering an awareness that we are still contributing and valuable members of society. It is necessary that we feel this way if we are to be happy.

Some women who would prefer to work a little now and then are kept from it because they don't know how to go about getting a job. Even if you've never worked before, it's quite possible to find something you are capable of doing and to get paid for doing it. I know quite a few older women who never worked outside their homes before, who are now working part-time and making a little extra money to supplement their Social Security and whatever other income they have.

Most older people will want to work only part time. Those who prefer to work full-time will try to stay with their jobs as long as possible or else get another full-time, less-demanding job when mandatory retirement catches up with them.

Office Work

Business women would seem to have the edge over the rest of us when it comes to working part-time or temporarily. If they want only temporary work, they can go to one of the employment agencies specializing in providing temporary help, take a test, and wait for the phone to ring. Neither the agency nor most employers seem to care how old a temporary employee is so long as she can do the work.

If skills are rusty from disuse, it might pay to take some kind of volunteer job where business and office skills are required and polish up your skills for nothing. It might also pay to take a short brush-up course at a business school, or rent a typewriter and practice for a month or two.

Clerking

Clerking in a store part-time or during the rush season is a job that many older women enjoy. Often, one will be expected to work evenings, week-ends, or odd hours, but when one is working temporarily, the hours are not all that important.

Baby-Sitting

Baby-sitting is another thing that older women do. Many people prefer the grandmotherly type, they tell me. One finds these jobs by looking in the want-ad section of the paper or by contacting an agency specializing in finding and placing baby sitters. The pay is not great, but the work is not hard if you like children. If you do not enjoy children, this type of work is not for you. Of course, some children are easier to manage than others, but a good baby-sitter can be rather selective.

If you enjoy children and your income is very low, it might be well to find out if there is a Foster Grandparents program in your area. I know a woman who really enjoys her work with retarded children in a program of this kind. She works under rather close supervision with only one or two children at a time. It's much easier, she says, than going out by the day or hour to baby-sit in a strange place and to be completely responsible. Even if there is no program in your area, it might be possible to find such a job as an aide in a nursery school or as an assistant baby-sitter during church services or at a bowling alley or tennis club.

Sitting with the Elderly

Personally, I find it much easier to "sit" with elderly persons who need someone with them at all times. I stay occasionally with a blind lady when her son's wife goes out for the day or afternoon, or when the couple go away on a week-end. A friend who no longer wanted the job referred me to the couple. One such job will lead to another. People tell other people about their finds.

Selling Your Skills to Others

If you have a special skill or talent of any kind, you can put it to work making money. I know a wonderful old lady past eighty who was a housewife and a homemaker all her life—and a good one. Now that she is old and widowed and living alone in a high-rise apartment built specifically for the not-too-affluent elderly, she's still doing what she knows best —and making money at it.

No doubt, activity has kept her in good health and in good shape, and she "helps out" the other old ladies who are not so active and strong as she. She cleans their apartments for only $1.50 an hour—she works for this because she is somewhat slower than she used to be. However, she makes fifteen or twenty extra dollars a week this way. Many of the older people in the building are too feeble to clean their apartments properly, and they are delighted to have her inexpensive and cheerful help.

She also runs errands; she will go to the drugstore, the post office, the supermarket, or to pay bills for a small fee. Though past eighty, she is providing a service that is needed at a price people can afford—the secret of most successful business operations.

Another woman in the building does alterations. Another one bakes and sells her baked goods—cakes, pies, bread, cookies, and delicious homemade egg noodles. Sometimes she bakes on order; sometimes she bakes things and sells them by the slice or half dozen.

I know another older woman who lives in a retirement home for rich old ladies who does beautiful handwork—all kinds of embroidery and quilting and crochet. She takes orders and makes things for about two dollars an hour, plus the cost of materials. It gives her something to do and gives her extra spending money.

Another who still lives in her own house sells African violets, herbs, and other plants of all kinds, which she grows under artificial light in her basement.

Selling Handicrafts

If you sew well or do nice handwork or crafts of any kind, you can either make things to sell directly to others or put them on consignment to be sold at a craft shop. You won't make very much, but you will make a little.

I worked temporarily as a bookkeeper-clerk at a handicraft shop where all the items were made by handicapped and elderly people, and the things that sold best were stuffed toys and dolls, pillows, and inexpensive crocheted items. One woman made covered hangers; another crocheted and stuffed baby blocks which sold like hotcakes. Still another made beautiful and unusual stationery by punching out colored dots with a paper punch and pasting them in place on inexpensive store-bought paper.

Teaching

If you do anything or know anything well, you can teach it to others for a price—ceramics, cake decorating, bridge, bread making, sewing, painting, tatting, crochet, a foreign language, or yoga. I have paid to learn to do many of these things, and many of the instructors were older people.

Nobody cares how old you are if you are competent, alert, and reasonably well preserved. Exquisite grooming makes your appear younger than you are. Work on yourself and your clothes before you go out to get a job teaching your skill. Contact the places where these types of classes are offered—adult education centers, YMCA and YWCA, craft shops, or department stores.

Strictly At-Home Work

If you prefer to work solely at home, go to the library and get some books on ways to make money at home. If you have difficulty in locating these books, ask the librarian for help. These books will describe how other people are making money at home; some people are engaged in activities you never even thought of.

Finding an Outside Job

If you decide that you would like to work part-time in a job outside, you must first decide what skills and services you have to offer and what you can and will enjoy doing. A bit of prior planning and preparation saves hours of frustration and footwork. Begin with a list of everything you have ever done since adolescence, every job you've ever had, and everything you know how to do. You will be amazed at how many things you can still do and how much you know.

Most of us who are old and poor cannot be too fussy about

what we do; we can no longer command high salaries. This is unfortunate but true. In fact, no one else wants the little jobs we will take—that's why we can usually find one. Most of us will not want to lose our Social Security incomes anyway, so we will settle for the low-paying part-time or temporary jobs that others pass by.

Once you have arrived at this realistic decision, take your neat little resumé, listing all former employment and all your skills, to the employment agencies that do not require a fee from you, and make an appointment to speak with a counselor. The state employment office is a good place to start; then try the job centers; and then the commercial agencies, including those that provide temporary office help, household help, and baby-sitting services. Try them all before you decide on anything.

Even if you do not think you would be interested in some of these jobs, see what is available. A friend of mine who had no outside work experience at all went to an agency and was hired immediately as a demonstrator. She works several days a week demonstrating cookware and thoroughly enjoys it. Another got a job reading to a blind student.

Watch the ads in the local paper, and respond to anything remotely suitable. The responding will give you practice in job hunting. Don't be discouraged by a few rebuffs.

Put your own ad in the paper in the "Situations Wanted" column. When a friend of mine gets ready to work, she puts in several ads at one time. One of them may read "Woman wants typing at home"; another reads "Woman wants part-time or temporary work. Experienced clerk and office worker." Don't mention age. There will be time for that when you go for the interview.

Tell everyone you know that you are available and looking for part-time or temporary work. The more people you have helping you, the greater the chance you have of getting something that suits you.

Part-time work will often seem to fall into your lap when people know you are looking. I decorated a bedroom closet for a relative; I covered boxes, hangers, and made shelf edgings and other closet accessories from a pair of pretty sheets. A friend of hers saw it and engaged me to similarly renovate her closets for a nice little fee. I have worked on a number of closets since, and it is work I enjoy, but I would never have thought of trying to get a job doing this.

Don't be reluctant to take temporarily a job that doesn't seem to be exactly what you had in mind—sometimes these work out very well. Since it's only part-time or temporary, it won't last forever, and you'll have money enough for a trip or a little luxury. Try to get a reference when the job ends. Give them your best.

Barter

Sometimes you'll find a job where there is no money involved. You give services or skills to people who give you something you need in return.

Two or three times a year I go in and clean the cupboards and closets of a beauty operator I know. I also repair her clothes, mend and patch and fix hems, and do odds and ends that working women never seem to have time for. In exchange she gives me a haircut, permanent, manicure, and pedicure which would cost me fifty dollars if I paid for these services. Occasionally I clean her apartment in exchange for a haircut and a manicure. Another woman, a former accountant, keeps the beautician's books for her and does her income tax in exchange for beauty services.

Once or twice a month, I go to the country to stay over the weekend with the teenage children of a rural couple who go away Friday afternoon and return on Sunday evening. In exchange for my services, they give me honey, milk, eggs, cream, and meat from their freezer and fresh fruit and vegetables in season. I usually do some baking, cleaning, or can-

ning and preserving for them on Saturday, but this is work
I thoroughly enjoy. I also enjoy the children, who are charming and agreeable.

I have a friend who tutors a little boy in reading in exchange for free tickets and transportation to the show. His
father manages the theater.

Knowing many people is a big help if you are interested in
barter. Talk with people; listen to them; don't be hesitant
about offering your services. You may find this old-fashioned
barter very rewarding, as I do. No money changes hands,
but it enables one to live much more nicely on nearly nothing. It's an ideal way for the older person to make life more
pleasant for herself—and for others.

Even when unemployment is at an all-time high, it's still
possible for an alert, active older woman to find a job whenever she wants one. It does take initiative, determination, per-
sistence, and courage—and usually some compromise on your
part—but the paycheck in your hand is your reward.

18.

In Pursuit
of Happiness

Old age should be a good time of life, perhaps the best time. Many of the internal emotional problems that blocked happiness in our younger years have been resolved. Many of the things that disturbed us and that seemed so important when we were younger no longer matter—we can dismiss them now as trivia. We are now ready for long periods of utter peace, contentment, and joy.

Happiness is an individual matter—there are different routes to it—but it is an ultimate goal for all of us. Perhaps it wasn't always, but it is now.

Happiness has nothing to do with money or the lack of it, although I recall the comment of that magnificent lady of song who said, "I've been poor and I've been rich—and rich is better." I heartily concur, but being rich does not guarantee happiness—although I am sure it would help some.

But poverty and unhappiness are not spelled the same either. You *can* be happy, though poor and old. So how do you go about it?

Part of the problem people seem to have in the pursuit of happiness is that they believe there are things outside themselves that would make them happy if they could just lay hold of them; they simply wait for happiness to happen; they don't see happiness as something they can do.

But, there are things you can do—attitudes to acquire; false fears and worries to eliminate; erroneous beliefs to get rid of; all sorts of things to *do* in order to achieve the happiness, serenity, and the occasional exuberant joy to which you are entitled. Your own personal happiness is now the first priority of your life and worth working for. So how do you begin?

Get Involved in Something That Interests You

To be happy you must be involved—either with people, or with work, or with activities meaningful to you. Many of us, for the first time in our lives, now have the leisure and time to engage in these activities and this work, to cultivate the people with whom we can relate. Ideally, this involvement should tap our inner resources and our creativity and thus lead to personal growth and fulfillment.

It is a continuing involvement with life and a continuing effort to learn, to achieve, and to grow that keeps us vital and happy. The talented and brilliant have an easier time with involvement, I'm sure. Can you imagine Helen Hayes or Margaret Mead ever giving up? But, one does not need to be intellectually inclined or talented, or even very bright, to continue to grow, to learn, and to be involved. People get involved in life by working in a garden, sewing, reading, taking walks, looking at paintings, listening to music, talking with people, having a social life, making new friends, traveling, doing volunteer work, taking care of a favorite grandchild, pursuing a second career, or doing anything else they find pleasure in.

Women probably have an easier time with involvement than men. Many men have had only their jobs—no hobbies, no consuming interests other than their work—and when mandatory retirement comes, what else is left for them to do but die? So they do, many of them, or they wander around like lost souls, not knowing what to do with themselves, often quite miserable in retirement. In contrast to this are people who have planned their retirement, who know what they are going to do, and who look forward eagerly to doing what has been planned.

Reach back into your past. What were your dreams and aspirations? What was it that you always wanted to do but never had time for? What was it that you never quite got around to or that the press of circumstances prevented? Do it now.

I know a woman who never finished high school and who wanted to go to college. For some reason known only to herself she wanted a college degree. She got one at seventy-two. She fulfilled a lifelong ambition after she was widowed, after her children were grown and taken care of, and after she had earned and saved enough money to educate herself.

I know of women who have begun exciting second careers after retirement—an early retirement in most cases. One of them has a handcraft shop; one of them runs her own secretarial service; another operates a baby-sitting bureau; another has a reducing business. All of them tell me they work harder at managing their own businesses than they did at their run-of-the-mill jobs, but that they enjoy it much more.

Sometimes these second careers turn out to be real money-makers, and, if so, that's all to the good too! A friend with a flair for decorating became a full-fledged decorator after retirement and makes more than she ever did at her former job.

I know a man who retired from his small-college teaching post to write textbooks on sociology and anthropology and has made more on his books than he did in years of teaching.

All things are possible, but making a pot of money isn't the main and only goal. I know a couple who retired early, built

their own boat—he was a carpenter—and against the advice
of absolutely everyone, sailed out to see the world. They've
been doing this for years now on very little money, and they
love it. They've had some fascinating and ghastly experiences
in out-of-the-way waters and exotic ports all over the world.
This is their fulfillment of a dream. This, for them, is happiness.

Don't Dwell on the Past

Most of us have things in our past that bring us pain. We
have done things and said things we wish we hadn't said and
done. At times we have been foolish, cruel, selfish, vicious,
thoughtless, or stupid. Guilt feelings about past mistakes and
failures can make us completely miserable in our old age if
we dwell on them, now that we have time to do so.

Don't permit yourself guilt. Excuse yourself, justify yourself, analyze and understand yourself, or do whatever is necessary to forgive yourself. And assume that others you have
wronged or have not treated well forgive you too.

Then you can resolve to do better. Knowing all that you
know now, it's much easier to be kind, tolerant, loving,
understanding, strong, gracious, and charming than it used to
be.

I know a woman of seventy who insists on punishing herself with guilt because she didn't treat her mother well. She
didn't, of course, but her mother was not an easy one to
treat well. Had she permitted it, her mother would have
completely dominated and ruled her life in the name of love.

I know a man who feels a complete failure at sixty-five because he was not able to accomplish and achieve what he
set out to do. Ill health plagued him most of his life; all things
considered, he did quite well, but he cannot see and accept
this.

I know a woman who refuses to forgive herself because at
sixteen she gave away an illegitimate child and still tortures

herself with remembering. There really wasn't anything else she could have done at the time, but she cannot accept this fact.

These people are dredging up their pasts to make themselves miserable in their old age. They refuse to understand and forgive themselves. They keep going over and over their unfortunate pasts like a rat running a maze.

Some older people with happier pasts like to go back and remember the good old days, which is a mistake too. The good old days weren't really all that good, if the truth be known, and this, too, keeps us from living in the present where we belong.

I have a friend who keeps remembering the happy times she had with her husband. She wishes back and yearns back in nostalgia instead of getting involved in the present. She recalls the trips they took together, the many friends they enjoyed, and the beautiful parties they gave, instead of attempting to cope with her present state of aloneness. She uses nostalgia like a drug to dull and insulate herself from the present. She could take trips alone now; she could make friends; she could entertain; but she does none of these things because she is so busy dredging up her happy past, which does not make her happy now—only miserable.

If the past gives you pain, don't think about it or talk about it. Let it go. Live for and in the present. Become so involved in the present you don't have time to go back and remember the past. It's possible to almost erase an unhappy or unfortunate past, to dismiss it almost completely. You have to exercise some positive thought control and push the negative thoughts about the past out of mind. We all must take some responsibility for our emotional as well as our physical health.

How does one push unhappy thoughts out of mind? Meditation helps some people do this. Meditation tends to train one to push almost all thoughts aside momentarily. A friend of mine paid several hundred dollars to be trained in the art

of meditation, but many train themselves to meditate satisfactorily with a do-it-yourself approach found in a book from
the public library.

When I find myself dwelling unhappily on the past, I go
out for a long, brisk walk, and I get out where people are,
my cure for almost everything. This brings me back rather
quickly to the present.

A writer friend says she immediately gets involved in some
activity that requires intense mental concentration on her part
—heavy reading, gourmet cooking, conversation with an in-
tellectual friend, studying her foreign language lesson, or
plotting a new story.

I know another woman who simply moved away from her
unhappy and unfortunate past. She went away and left it,
physically and mentally. She took a new look at life and
started over in another and completely different area. "My
past is still back there," she says, "but I seldom think of it."

Most of us will not want or need to take such drastic
measures to come to terms with our past. We have only to
think of each day as a fresh beginning, as the first day of the
rest of our lives, and every day start over.

Get intensely involved in the present. Plan each day so that
you get and give some pleasure. Eventually the past will fade
and there will be only now, which is as it should be.

Don't Worry About the Future or Live in It

There are so many things for poor old people to worry
about. They worry about getting sick and having to go to a
nursing home, about not having enough money to take care
of themselves in their last years, about becoming senile and
dying, and on and on and on.

Everyone should, of course, make plans for the future—
this is not worry, but intelligent planning. You should think
out exactly what you are going to do in the event of catas-
trophe. You should have insurance. You should, if possible,
have a certain amount of money set aside for emergencies,

to take care of illness, and perhaps enough to get into a "home." But, anything above that set aside amount should be slowly spent on pleasure.

In the event you should have a very long and expensive illness, there is always welfare in addition to Medicare. You will be taken care of in some way. Our society does a fairly good job of providing for its elderly, and it may do even better in the years to come. Other people have already borne all the things that worry you, and if necessary, you will bear them too. So there is really nothing to worry about.

Worry is such a futile activity—it does absolutely no good and possibly much harm. Most of the things worriers concern themselves with never happen. If you are a worrier, you must somehow convince yourself of this. You must literally school yourself to stop worrying.

There are those who believe we actually bring into existence the things we dwell upon, that if we dwell upon misfortune, it will come. In any event, it is well to teach yourself a more positive attitude, more positive thinking. Again, it takes practice, but it can be done.

Sometimes worry is a defense mechanism—people worry to keep from having to do anything constructive. Sometimes it's easier that way. They prefer to immobilize themselves with worry so they won't have to make tough decisions and act upon them. If we are to be happy, we cannot let worry about the future spoil the present. Getting intensely involved in the present almost always precludes worrying about the future. There just isn't time.

Some people tend to postpone living until some future date when circumstances are right or different. They make elaborate plans for the future and ignore the present. So, the years go by, time slips away, and the future is seldom what they thought it was going to be.

I had a retired friend who lived in the future, ignoring the present. "I must have $50,000 in my savings account," she kept telling herself and me, "and then I will be able to travel

and get a color television and move into a nicer apartment
and enjoy my retirement." So she scrimped and saved
mightily from her more-than-adequate income and added to
her nest egg. Her future never came. Shortly before she
reached her goal, she died suddenly, and her hard-saved
money went to a nephew, who promptly blew it.

Living in the future and postponing all pleasure is almost
never a good idea, almost as unsatisfying as living in the past.
If you are one of those people who tend to postpone enjoyment and things that give you pleasure until some future date,
it is time to pull yourself up short and begin to enjoy life
now. We older ones must live for today. Tomorrow may never
come. The past is done; the future is uncertain; the time for
us is now.

Become a Sensuous Woman

Sharpen up your senses—learn to see, feel, hear, smell,
touch, and enjoy as if for the first time. Those whose senses
are finely tuned enjoy life more fully, experience all of life
with a heightened awareness, and often find an almost exquisite pleasure in simply being alive.

I had a blind friend who was enabled with surgery to see
again after years of sightlessness, and the joy she found in
just looking and seeing was startling and almost unbelievable.
She was completely enthralled by the junk jewelry display in
the dime-store window; a fat puppy waddling toward her
would send her into ecstasy; and the sight of a beautiful child
was almost more than she could bear. After being with her
for a brief time, I realized how jaded my own sense of sight
had become.

All our senses tend to dull with age in defense against the
constant clatter and batter of sound and sight. Most of our
lives are spent rushing about making a living, competing,
striving, hurrying to get to work, hurrying back home again,
and racing to get the chores done. We become so intent on
keeping things together that we don't have time to stop and

look and listen and touch and feel. Well, now there is time for all these things, time to enjoy the feel of things and the taste of things and the sound of things and little pieces of beauty hidden away in corners. This is the essence of happiness, and it is free for the taking. It doesn't cost a cent—all we have to do is reach out, and touch it, and take it.

With a bit of self-training and practice, we can learn to perceive with a new and heightened awareness. As you go about your daily chores and activities, do so with awareness. Don't let yourself go into anything dull, deaf, blind, and lethargic. Notice and think and listen; feel your reactions. It is feeling that you must become aware of. Ask yourself often, How does this make me feel? What am I feeling now?

A sensuous person lives more fully and intensely than others. She is closer to life, more fully tuned in. Even the simple act of taking a morning shower can become an experience if done with awareness. The sensuous one doesn't just take a shower —she feels with an exquisite awareness the hot pinpoints of water cascading over her, the feel of water stinging down on her upturned face, and the first, crisp, cool scent and splash of cologne dashed over her shoulders.

Likewise, the simple act of baking a loaf of bread can make a whole day special. You can revel in the heady smell of yeast and the swollen look of it as it rises in the little yellow bowl; you can enjoy the feel of the dough under your hands as you knead and pummel and the springy, almost-aliveness of the risen dough as you shape it into loaves. The smell of its baking fills your rooms, earthy and fragrant; and then you cut the first crusty slice from the brown-topped loaf and eat it, preferably with butter running down through your fingers, and the warm, coarse taste of it is something you'll never get from the corner grocery.

For ultimate enjoyment, the fresh loaf should be shared, of course, and it can be if you've had the forethought to invite someone in to a simple supper. Conversation and shared feelings of friendship and caring are to be savored, too, and linger on after the guest has gone. The day becomes lovely, all feeling and touching and smelling and tasting—and sharing.

We can all enjoy these things now. We have the time and leisure to let the senses go free and revel in the pleasure they bring.

As you work at sharpening up your senses and your perception, you will find yourself becoming more acutely and actively alive; you will find that you experience more and enjoy more; you will find greater pleasure in so many simple things—the feel of rain on your face, the crunch of snow underfoot, or just striding along with the wind in your hair.

You will find yourself looking for and finding pleasure in things other people never notice or take for granted: the beauty of a piece of glass as you hold it up to the window and polish it; the city's lights from the bedroom window; night and stars. Sometimes you will get up early to see the sun rise.

You will find yourself listening to the sound of music and the sounds of words going together with the same intense pleasure. The prose of Carl Sandburg and Eudora Welty become sheer poetry, as do some parts of the Bible, especially when read aloud to yourself from a rocking chair at midnight.

My children loved to take the hamster out of his cage and play with him in person. As the ultimate delight they would put him inside their shirts, and, feeling his warm furry little body, his nibbling and nudging against their naked skins, they would shiver and giggle in sheer ecstasy. I think about it now. This is the way to be a happy, sensuous woman, to figuratively put the hamster inside our shirts.

Don't Expect Other People to Make You Happy

Many older people seem to lean on their children for their happiness. They seek it only through and in their children and others, and when the younger people become engrossed in their own lives and pursuits, they often feel lonely and slighted.

This attitude is one of the greatest stumbling blocks to a happy old age. It keeps us from growing, from exploring new avenues of expression and creativity, and from becoming more of a person. It keeps us from seeking happiness where it really is—in ourselves.

A close, warm, loving relationship with one's adult children is to be desired (and valued if one has it), but we have only to look around us to see that a great many people don't. Very often there is not love but tolerance, and sometimes not even that. In-laws and other complications often preclude closeness, and, in this case, it may be well not to keep wishing and reaching for something that does not exist, but to accept the fact realistically and find joy and love elsewhere and on your own.

Likewise, we should not let other people keep us from our happiness and rob us of this right, either. Parents tend to let their children do this to them. Recently I heard an older woman say wistfully and quite sadly, "I have everything to make me happy. I could be so happy if it weren't for my son's drinking problem." His problem is unfortunate, of course, but her son is an adult and no longer her prime responsibility. If she is to be happy, she must let his problem go and not hold it to herself. There is nothing she can do about his problem. Unknowingly, perhaps, she helps him feed it rather than alleviate it, as is almost always the case when mothers become too involved in or too concerned about their adult children's problems. It is not intelligent to let another make us unhappy, even an adored child.

I have a neighbor who permits herself to be annoyed every afternoon by the daily visit of a sweet, boring little lady who calls promptly at two and stays until five. My neighbor maintains she cannot tell this old friend that she often prefers to rest and read.

One has to be strong and realistic and ever so slightly hardboiled to survive and be happy in this world of the aged. We are responsible for ourselves and ourselves alone. We alone are responsible for our own good times. We must not look to others to make us happy and then blame them or feel hurt and put upon when they don't. It is a mistake to expect anyone else to give you the key to the kingdom of happiness. It is impossible for them to give it to you, because you already have it in your own hand.

Do Only What You Want to Do and What You Enjoy Doing

I have friends who serve on committees, who take charge of things, who are presidents and chairwomen of things, and who make countless telephone calls and do dozens of things they don't enjoy doing because they think they *should*. If you enjoy doing these things—and there are many people who do —then you certainly should do them. But, if you don't enjoy them, there are probably enough other people around to get them done. Of course, you must be able to shrug off the disagreeable chores without any guilt feelings whatsoever. It helps to remember that you are making some contributions by doing the things you do enjoy.

Why go to meetings that bore you? Why continue to join a club you've belonged to for years when you are no longer interested? Why go to church because you've always gone? Why do things because other people expect you to? Why contribute money to worthy causes when you have so little for yourself? Why give expensive gifts to others? Do you prefer to volunteer your services to some worthy cause or go out and get some little part-time job and get paid for working? Why baby-sit with bratty grandchildren so their parents can have a night out or a month's vacation?

If you enjoy baby-sitting with grandchildren, either adorable or otherwise, of course you should do it. Then it's a pleasure. You should probably also baby-sit occasionally even if you don't enjoy it, if your son-in-law has recently painted your kitchen ceiling. If you take, you have to give. He probably didn't enjoy the ceiling very much either.

When we were working and raising our families, there were so many things we *had* to do. But now it is time to conclude that you do not have to do anything you do not want to do. Once this decision has been reached, you will know a wonderful sense of freedom that is akin to joy.

Get in the Habit of Doing Many Things You Like to Do Alone

This is something that can be learned, and it's necessary to learn it if you would have a happy old age. The older we get, the more alone we will become. This is a simple fact of life. Friends die, become decrepit, and move away. Acquaintances wander off. Relatives become involved in their own lives and with other people. But the person who has learned to enjoy aloneness and the pleasure of her own company will never be unhappy or lonely just because she is alone. We must look forward to much aloneness and see to it that the hours are filled with pleasure.

It came as something of a shock when my friends began to deteriorate physically and could no longer do and enjoy the things we used to do and enjoy together. Rather than stay home or be bored with things I didn't enjoy, I had to plunge out alone. At first I hated it, then I didn't mind, and now I enjoy it.

I walk for miles alone. I go look-shopping alone once a week and I go to church, to the library, to the store, and even for a picnic in the park—alone. The people that I knew do not any more enjoy the activities that I do—and some of them are gone. I don't enjoy bridge, games, television, old-lady gossip, or walking like a snail. When I shop, I wear everybody down, so I go alone and have learned to like it. So must everyone who intends to have a happy old age.

It's also a good idea to learn to enjoy some solitary sedentary activities that require no one else's company—reading, handwork, keeping a journal, making scrapbooks, puttering about in the house, working crossword puzzles, solitaire, crochet, or whatever else appeals to you—something to fill the hours happily when it becomes more difficult to get out and around.

There will be many hours of aloneness in the years ahead; they are good hours when you know what to do with them. Many times aloneness proves to be a blessing. It gives us an opportunity to become acquainted with ourselves in a deeper way and gives us insight, an opportunity to look within and find out who and what we are at this stage in time, so that we can make the most of what's left us.

Aloneness is no cause for unhappiness. There is a great big world still out there waiting to be explored alone.

Be Interested in Other People

An interest in others keeps us from becoming too intensely wrapped up in ourselves and in our own tight little world. You can get out of your rut, if you want to, with only a little effort. You don't even need to like people to be profoundly and passionately interested in them.

However, most of us need some other caring people in our lives to be happy. Perhaps a loner doesn't—and sometimes the loner is very happy in her own special way—but it is not the way for most of us. Most of us want desperately some closeness and caring.

To have friends, you must first meet them and then be courageous enough to take the initiative for friendship. When you are new in a strange place—or not new, but have made a new resolve—how do you go about meeting people? You go where they are. You walk down the street. You join a senior citizens' group. You take a class. You volunteer for something. You attend an AARP meeting. You join a club. You sign up for a trip with a group. You go to church. You talk with people while you wait for the bus or when going up and down in the elevator.

People are everywhere, needing you as much as you need

them. The years have given you something, so surely you must have something to give to others. Friendship is both giving and getting, both sharing and caring; otherwise, the relationship is hollow and unrewarding and might better be dissolved.

People are all around you. Reach out. If you are warm and outgoing, they tend to respond in kind. Even if you are shy and awkward around people, there is always a soul mate or two stuck away somewhere, if you care enough to ferret them out.

Once you've met some people and have some friendships in the offing, juggle your food budget so you can entertain occasionally. Entertaining seems to cement friendship, and it is another thing to be enjoyed. Entertaining need not be expensive. You can have an inexpensive tea or a pot luck party. You can invite someone to a salad supper, to a Sunday morning breakfast, or to a picnic in the park, even if you're not prepared for more elaborate entertaining. Often, these little impromptu get-togethers are more fun than the elaborate kind.

You can take this interest in people a step farther if you care to. Every day, do a little something for somebody, say something that cheers and pleases, run an errand, make a telephone call, or write a sincere note to a friend afar. Do something that will, perhaps for just a moment, give someone a little lift or a bit of pleasure.

Doing something for others tends to give us a good feeling about ourselves, a little feeling of worth and value, which is essential for a happy survival. So even when done for this purely selfish reason alone, it's good. But don't expect anything in return, or you've blown it! Many times people do return kindnesses, and, by accepting favors and compliments graciously, you permit them to feel good about themselves too. If you consciously give a little of yourself to others for awhile, it becomes a habit. You will do it without thinking, and people will probably find you a charming old woman.

Sometimes, when I feel the need for instant companionship, I make it a point to engage perfect stangers in conversation. If you don't know many people intimately, this is an easy way to keep yourself from feeling lonely and completely isolated from the rest of the world. Expect some rebuffs—some people don't want to talk—but many of them do, especially older ones.

Only yesterday, I had a delightful conversation with a grandmotherly type on the bus bench. On another day, I stopped to pass the time of day with an old man who sits on a porch, and he told me about his work as a Rock Island Railroad engineer. Talking, his face lighted up and he seemed to come to life before my eyes; he took on strength and color and sureness, almost as if a train whistle had blasted him suddenly alive.

Learn to take pleasure in making others happy, even if only for a moment. Often it takes no more than a word, a flicker of interest, or a trace of compassion.

Learn to Cope with Your Problems

Everyone has problems. Some people seem to have more than others, and some problems are bigger than others, but we all have them. It's a sign that we are still alive. It's what we do with them, how we cope with them, that makes the difference between being happy and unhappy.

Life is not a bed of roses at any age—do not expect it to be. The world is not run for the benefit of the elderly. We will always have problems and temporary unpleasantnesses, but when we bring everything we have to bear on these challenges that life continues to present, we grow stronger and smarter.

Problems are best faced head-on, not brushed under the rug so you can get them out every day or two and worry them anew like a dog with a bone. Incessant mulling over problems instead of facing them and taking appropriate action keeps one in a continual state of upset that is not conducive to peace of mind. It can also send your blood pressure rocketing.

To cope with a problem, enumerate all possible choices, and then decide what seems to be the best possible course of action for you. Then, take the action you have decided upon. *Do* something to or with the problem, or don't do anything, if that has been your decision. Once you have made your decision, let it be—don't mull it over any longer. The chances are, your first choice was the best possible course open to you. Time may prove otherwise, but we all make mistakes, and even mistakes are healthier than permanent indecision.

Denying that a problem exists is not a very satisfactory solution, as a rule. But sometimes, delaying it is effective. One problem at a time is all that I can handle. I delay the others while I'm coping with the most pressing, and sometimes the others disappear while I'm working on the first one. What seems like a problem today may not be a problem six months from now. Time may have diluted and fragmented it into nothingness.

Always Have Something to Look Forward To

Plan your life; plan your days and weeks, next month, and next year so you have something to look forward to with pleasure. It need not be anything elaborate—a family dinner, a little tea, a potluck party, making and putting up the Christmas decorations, a weekend away, a visit with an old friend, or a granddaughter's wedding. It makes no difference what the occasion is, just so that you can look forward to it with pleasure.

I plan little trips well in advance so that I have time to look forward to them. When I return from a longer trip, I immediately start planning another one so that I have a whole year to think about it and get ready for it.

I know people who send off for things from the mail order catalogs, who subscribe to magazines, and who write innumerable letters to pen pals they have never seen, just so they can look forward to getting their mail every day. With so much prior preparation, they are seldom disappointed by an empty box.

To anticipate is a child's trait, and it makes us all feel younger and happier. It keeps us from looking back and wishing back. It keeps us always going forward into life.

Take Care of Your Health

Health has much to do with happiness when one is older. It's difficult, if not impossible, to be happy when you're hurting or when you're ailing and feeling poorly. Those of us who still have our health and our mobility realize how fortunate we are. Some people who do not experience optimum health might possibly eat and exercise their way to better health, if they would just begin. When you are older, you cannot violate the rules for good health and stay healthy. Preserve your health by taking care of yourself and by using moderation in all things. Don't become a drunk or a drug addict out of pain or boredom.

A good doctor with all the medication at his disposal can do a lot to keep the ailing and aged comfortable enough to enjoy life. If you don't have a doctor who seems concerned about your discomfort, find one who does. Don't suffer more than you must.

With increasing age, we must be prepared for a certain amount of physical deterioration. We must all accept eventually the facts of aging—the wrinkles, the sag, the thinning hair, the inability to get around, and even the aches and pains when they appear.

I recently read an account of the last interview with an aging actress who could not realistically accept aging; it was a tragic story of a woman trying desperately but futilely to cling to youth and beauty. She failed eventually, of course, as everyone must. Her self-esteem seemed to be based largely upon the way she looked, an unfortunate basis for anyone past forty. Preserving herself and presenting an appearance of youth and beauty to the public seemed to be the all-consuming interest of her later years. In spite of all the money and material things she had accumulated, she came off as a very unhappy person.

In sharp contrast, for example, was noted anthropologist Margaret Mead, whose character and brilliance shone forth from her rather plain and frankly aging face. With nondescript hair and a plump little figure, she was far too busy, too interested, and too interesting to be overly concerned about how she looked; she was probably the most widely admired woman in the country, until her recent death.

Old people often have a need to see themselves as worn out, exhausted, used up, helpless, sick, and with all their resources depleted. They have given up on themselves and have given up on life. Though, sometimes they childishly resort to these tactics to get sympathy and attention. This seldom works very long—others get bored with helplessness and tired of whining.

Gutsy old ladies never do this, of course. They know they are never done until they are dead. Deep within them is an untapped well of strength, waiting to be called upon when needed.

Fix Up Your Living Quarters

No one can be happy living in squalor and discomfort and clutter. Recently, I visited a very unhappy older woman, not a particularly poor one either, in a very depressing apartment. The shades dropped over bare windows; unpacked cardboard boxes were stacked in the corners. Mess and clutter were everywhere. She apologized for the way the place looked, saying that since she had taken it only temporarily and was looking for another apartment, she saw no reason for unpacking. Making conversation, I asked her how long she had been there. She said six years. No wonder she was unhappy! Anyone would have become unhappy after six years in those surroundings.

Any place looks better if it is neat and shining clean. In fact, not even the poshest room with the most beautiful rugs and drapes and furniture looks attractive when dirty and cluttered. It's difficult to keep a small place neat and clean unless it's organized. So make places to put your belongings properly away, and get rid of things you no longer have any use for. Organization, utilizing all your space to advantage, is the key to keeping a small place looking neat and attractive.

Old people should have growing things, living things, and beautiful things around them. They keep us from feeling lonely when alone and shut in, and they give us something to do and to watch and care for. We should make an effort to gather things around us that we can enjoy when alone.

I would love to have a little dog to keep me company and to look after, but one cannot keep a dog comfortably in an apartment, so I have goldfish. I get no end of enjoyment from George and Gladys swimming incessantly in their little bowl. I enjoy plants and growing things, my herb garden, the things I've made, and the few beautiful things I've collected on my travels. These things give me pleasure every time I look at them. They are simple things, but I have learned to enjoy simple things. I no longer have expensive tastes or yearnings —and neither does anyone else who is happy though poor.

Get Rid of Everything Ugly

Discard your ugly old clothes, the robe you hate to be seen in, the worn and faded bathroom rug, the depressing half-dead plant, the cushion you made twenty years ago, the tattle-tale grey dresser scarf, the spread that has seen better days, and that awful picture your cousin brought from Portugal. Don't live with ugliness or things that are dirty, tattered, faded, or torn or that you dislike. It's depressing, especially when you are old and living alone.

Make new covers for your heating pad and ironing board; touch up the battered bureau; put some pretty paper around your cardboard storage boxes. Fix up your closets so they open to brightness and beauty instead of mess and clutter. Line the bureau drawers and shelves with pretty paper and edgings. These things cost practically nothing, and sometimes nothing at all.

The shelves in my kitchen cabinets and cupboards were dingy and chipped and ugly. They gave me a twinge every time I opened the door. I got a vinyl wallpaper book, free for the asking, cut the pages in squares and pasted them with homemade paste over the shelves and in the drawers.

I covered the tin cans that hold my do-it-yourself supplies with tiny, leftover scraps of material pasted on in a hit-and-miss fashion and made a shelf edging to match, pasting the scraps on thicknesses of newspaper for my storage cabinet. I put some little calico skirts around my ugly clay plant pots. Only a bit of work changed the look from ugly to gay freshness, and it didn't cost a thing.

When you keep your rooms fresh and bright and shining, you tend to feel the same way. Most of us take on color from our surroundings.

Don't Sit with Unhappiness or Depression

Everyone has days or moments of depression, low days when life's futility washes over one. Expect these periods occasionally. But don't sit and nurse them and let them jell into permanence. Get up and force yourself to do something, preferably somthing physical. That is the time to throw on a coat and take a long walk, or go for a swim, or get on the bus and ride to the end of the line and back again. Or clean the cupboards and drawers, or the whole house, if need be.

Or, try on all the clothes in your closet with the shoes, stockings, underwear, and accessories you plan to wear with them, and see what repairing or making over needs to be done. If nothing needs to be done, congratulate yourself and enjoy the way you look. Or, work on yourself—wash your hair, do your nails—then put on your makeup and a beautiful caftan and relax in the rocking chair with a good book.

Count Your Blessings Instead of
Dwelling on Your Lacks

Get in the habit of thankfulness. Be thankful for what you have, for little things as well as big things, and don't dwell on what you don't have.

Every morning I get up, thankful that I no longer have to go out to work; thankful for my safe, clean, comfortable little nest that I can pay for; thankful that I am healthy and strong and able enough to do whatever I want to do, and that I still have things I want to do; and thankful that most of my contacts with people are pleasant, and that some of them treat me kindly. After a short session such as this, the day is almost bound to start well, go well, and be gone before you're ready to have it end.

Treat Yourself to the Things You Want—
As Many as You Can Possibly Afford

It may be necessary to save on other things so you can have these treats. I save strenuously for my trips away. I save in order to buy myself presents when I feel blue or depressed. One Christmas my plans went awry at the very last moment, and I felt lost and low. I took all my house and gift money for the next six months and blew it on myself in one grand spree; I bought myself a beautiful pair of red shoes, a cake cover, an orange mixing bowl, a fancy skillet, a cutting scissors, and some odds and ends I'd been planning to get eventually anyway. Then I stacked them under a Christmas tree and had a beautiful Christmas, complete with decorations and dinner. In fact, I had such a nice time that I have, from choice, repeated this Christmas several times over. Gifts you buy yourself are often the very best kind.

Practice Not Being Upset by Trivia

I've seen and heard old ladies become completely unnerved because the TV repairman didn't come when he promised, or the groceries weren't delivered on time, or they had to get peaches when they wanted plums, or the hairdresser didn't fix their hair to suit, or someone slighted them or said an unkind thing.

You have to learn to roll with the jabs that other people give you, intentional or not, and to dismiss trivia for what they are. When you find yourself becoming annoyed or wrought up, ask yourself, What difference does this make? If it's going to matter six months from now or even six weeks from now, it may be worth losing your equilibrium over. But most of the little inconveniences and annoyances are going to evaporate into thin air in a day or two. Let them disappear while you concern yourself with things that really matter.

Make Friends with Yourself

Most people need friends—a few good friends, perhaps one best friend—but sometimes when one is old and does not get around too well, it is difficult to make new friends to replace those who have gone on.

Maybe you've been friends with yourself for a long time, and if so, you are one of the fortunate ones. But perhaps you never had the time or the inclination to become acquainted with yourself, your real inner self. Now there is time. Now you can concentrate on yourself, on learning to like yourself and respect yourself instead of spending so much time on and with others. When you nurture and counsel and comfort yourself properly, you will find that you can enjoy yourself and treat yourself the way you've always treated your other good friends—by being kind, considerate, loving, forgiving, understanding, and gentle.

This does not mean that you shouldn't be tough with yourself occasionally. Real friends often are—they stimulate us to be our own best selves and bring out the best in us. So you must be tough enough to see that you do what you should —for your own good, of course—that you eliminate bad habits and wrong ways of thinking and doing that keep you from the happiness and the things you desire and deserve. You must be tough enough to keep yourself at the things you've started.

But never make yourself miserable or unhappy by dwelling on your age or your shortcomings and inadequacies. Analyze and categorize them instead. Then separate them neatly into three groups: (1) Those you cannot possibly do anything about, such as disability or age (dismiss them—think no more about them); (2) Those you *can* do something about (get to work on them immediately and permit no slipups and no excuses); and (3) Those you *could* do something about but that do not bother you unduly (ignore them).

Do not continually grind yourself down because you are old or because of your flaws and shortcomings. Concentrate on the things you can still do rather than those you can't. Concentrate on the things in yourself that are good and fine and splendid. Look for them—when you see them, others will too. Approve of yourself. Can you actually admire yourself? When you really do, others will too. But, others are not so important to you now, and they will become less so.

We are so accustomed to waiting for others to give us a kind word or to do us a good deed that we never think of doing these things for ourselves. Why? We know better than anyone else when we need comfort, encouragement, solace, or advice. So, be kind to yourself, be loving.

Consider Religion and Polishing Up Your Faith

Many people find joy in a renewed or continuing faith. These later years offer an opportunity to enhance spiritual well-being. Now that there is more time, it seems only natural to spend some of it concentrating on things of the spirit. After fifty or more years' experience in living, many people have come to a recognition of the need to place trust in a power beyond themselves.

There should be no attempt to inflict one's preferences or beliefs on others. A faith that satisfies is something that each person must seek and find alone. However, to enhance happiness, faith must create joy. There are those who pretend to live by and in faith who are merely pious, long-suffering, and long faced. One has a feeling that these people have put their trust in something that is not real and not true. Real faith brings us closer to joy, strength, courage, serenity, and peace —all the things we older ones must have to endure, to survive, and to be happy.

19.

How to Be a Shut-In and Enjoy Life

Any one of us could become a shut-in, and sooner or later, many of us probably will. For those of us who are alone, the alternative to staying in our own place is to go to a nursing home—where the care may be adequate, indifferent, or downright poor, depending to a certain extent on the price we can afford to pay.

You must be ambulatory to get into most retirement homes, you must have sufficient money to make the initial payment, and your monthly income must be sufficient to cover the cost of maintenance there. This precludes many of us. So it's either a nursing home, with some help from welfare to pay for it, or our own little place.

Is it possible to stay in your own place and manage your own life, and yet enjoy it when you can't get out and around? To find out, I talked with two women who do. One woman, who gets about slowly and painfully with a walker, hasn't been outside her apartment building in years, but she says she has learned to manage her life and her affairs efficiently and happily. The other maintains that the only problem she has is with her family. Her family would prefer to have her in a nursing home, she says, and occasionally she finds it necessary to shout them down.

Families usually prefer "homes" for us, because it relieves them of responsibility, allays their guilt feelings (if any), and gets us out of their way so they don't have to concern themselves with looking after us. Looking after an old person can become a real chore, so we must learn to look after ourselves if we intend to maintain ourselves in our own place. We must retain independence and autonomy, and resist letting family and friends coerce and influence us in making decisions that affect us and our happiness.

The women that I visited convinced me that if you are not so ill as to require constant nursing care, it is possible to maintain oneself in one's own place and be much happier than in a nursing home. You have to be able to get in and out of bed by yourself and to manage to go to the bathroom by yourself. These would seem to be the criteria. If you can do these two things, you can manage alone if you know how, if you have initiative and determination, and if you keep your faculties sharpened up.

Society is presently encouraging the elderly to stay out of nursing homes and in their own places by providing free or low cost services that enable them to do so. A nurse comes in to check on both the ladies once a week. Both have free household help. A houseworker comes in once a week to clean their places, to do their washing and ironing, and to take care of other necessary chores.

Meals on Wheels is a program that provides two meals a day brought to the door by volunteer workers. The recipient is charged whatever she can afford to pay. Friendly Neighbors provides a hot lunch five days a week in the basement of the low-cost apartment building where one of the ladies lives. She goes down to lunch every day that she can and enjoys the socialization that this interlude away from her own place provides.

It is still possible to find grocery stores that will deliver merchandise for a fee. The groceries are usually more expensive than those picked up personally from the supermarket shelves, but it is the only way a shut-in can manage; they are also very convenient in cold and rainy weather for those who are not shut in. It is well to order a quantity of groceries at one time to avoid paying a delivery fee every week. In fact, most stores will not deliver less than a twenty-dollar order. A shut-in should certainly plan meals in advance and make lists so that everything is available when needed.

Some fast-food places will deliver hot food to the door. One of the ladies says she orders fried chicken or pizza on weekends when Friendly Neighbors meals are not available. Milk, cheese, and other dairy products are delivered once a week.

Drugstores will deliver to the door if orders are phoned in; so will department stores if you have a charge account. Both of the ladies have doctors they've had for years who will prescribe for them over the phone.

Both of them pay all their bills and do all their shopping by mail. Even stamps may be ordered by mail from the post office.

If you explain your situation to big mail order houses, they will usually send their catalogs to you. It is possible to order almost everything you need from these catalogs without stepping out of the house. Their merchandise ranges from expensive to cheap. If it is not satisfactory, it can be returned, but you do have to wrap it up and get it ready for return and have it taken to the post office. Once you've ordered, and if you keep ordering occasionally, the catalogs will automatically be sent to you year after year.

Once you begin ordering, you will soon be on the list of smaller mail order firms, and your mailbox will be stuffed with their catalogs, from which you can order tempting little things for gifts, or gadgets for yourself.

Both the ladies have their Social Security and other checks sent to their banks. Since they pay all their bills and take care of other expenses by check, they require very little cash on hand. One of them tells me she sometimes has only a dollar or two in the house and gets cash only several times a year.

It is usually possible to find someone who will run errands, do little odds and ends, and help take care of your business for a price. One woman hires a dependable high school girl once a month. The other, who lives in an apartment building for the indigent elderly, is assisted by an active, alert older woman who lives in the building and runs errands for the others for a small fee. Occasionally other people will run errands for a shut-in, but one should be careful not to impose.

One of the women says that when you don't go out, you need only a few house clothes. What clothes she has are ordered by mail. If they must be altered, a woman in the building comes in to fix them. This woman also occasionally makes for her a garment that she calls a coat dress; it buttons down the front and is easy to get in and out of, an ideal garment for an arthritic shut-in.

If there is sufficient money, it's possible to have a beauty operator come in and fix your hair and give you a manicure and pedicure. If not, wear your hair long or short and cut it and fix it yourself, or wear a wig. A friend or relative can be a big help when it comes to your hair and nails.

Thus, it is possible to take care of all physical needs if you can get around in your own place. But, what does a shut-in do to enjoy life? How are the long days spent? What about entertainment?

There are, they tell me, reading and resting, television, solitaire, crossword puzzles, handwork, and an occasional game of Scrabble with someone across the way. Also, everything takes longer. One of them says it takes her at least an hour to dress and comb her hair, and another hour to prepare the simplest of breakfasts and wash the few dishes. It takes a good half day to clean and straighten the bureau drawers.

Both of them say they have come to terms with loneliness and actually enjoy aloneness now that they are at peace with themselves. Also, they enjoy everyone who comes in—the paper boy, the man who delivers the groceries, the telephone repairman, the milkman, the nurse, the housekeeper, the Avon lady, and the neighbors who drop in. Even a shut-in is not without some people contacts.

Both admit they are somewhat addicted to television and keep it on most of the day for company. One does embroidery, usually from kits, which she orders from various magazines and catalogs. It's easier this way, she says—the yarn, the needles, and the directions are all there. She gives the things she makes as Christmas gifts, as a rule. She also does handwork for a handcraft shop that handles the work of homebound handicapped and elderly people. The therapist brings the materials to her and picks up the finished work. It is sold in the shop to bring in a bit of extra spending money.

The public library has a service whereby books are delivered to shut-ins and picked up. Both of them take advantage of this service and read rather widely. The library will also send specially ordered books to them by mail. Talking books are sent through the mail to people with visual problems, a wonderful service for handicapped shut-ins and the blind.

Both the ladies tell me the bright spot of their day is getting their mail. It's something to be looked forward to and enjoyed. One of the women subscribes to as many magazines as she can afford, and she sends off coupons for free and inexpensive samples of everything she sees in the magazines. She says she even occasionally sends off to mail order and gift houses for things she doesn't really need. She has worlds of time to write letters and keeps up with family and old friends; her mail box is usually stuffed, the way she wants it.

They both keep journals, make scrapbooks, read the Bible, and meditate, all of which are activities that tend to keep one mentally alert and content. They even have people in to eat occasionally, ordering the food sent in.

The woman who lives in the apartment building for the elderly entertains with a simple tea once a month. She invites each of the people on the floor, a different one each month, to share tea and little cakes with her. It takes her a long time to prepare for it. She does it nicely with a bit of assistance from her neighbors, and she enjoys it. She used to entertain elaborately, she remembers.

Then there are friends who call, either in person or on the phone. As one gets older, fewer friends are left to call, and a shut-in does not get out to make new friends, so the calls become less frequent. There is a service in town, however, where a volunteer calls a designated number of shut-ins at about the same time every day. If there is no answer, someone is dispatched to the address to investigate. Thus, the outside world comes briefly into the life of the shut-in, a call indicative that someone, if only a volunteer, cares enough to keep in touch.

Both my friends not only subscribe to this service, but also volunteer to call others during the day, doing their bit to make the lives of other shut-ins a bit more pleasant.

A shut-in must have courage and be brave and completely without self-pity. If you are courageous enough and brave enough, you can enjoy life as a shut-in.

20.

Staving Off Senility

We may not be able to stave off genuine senility; a combination of physican and mental deterioration that may come just with living too long. But, we can stave off the appearance of it. What appears to be senility is often a collection of sloppy habits, poor attitudes, inactivity, and lack of involvement with life and with people.

We can't eliminate the fact of being old. We *are* old or are getting old, and we will all be older in time. What we can eliminate is old behavior, behavior that makes us appear decrepit, dull, dim-witted, and not with it. Who wants to be any of these things?

We can do something about these things. It behooves each of us to analyze our behavior, our attitudes, and our habits to determine what makes us look, act, and feel old and fuzzy headed and then to take steps to correct or eliminate whatever it is that makes us look and act and feel that way. Among them are little things and big things that most of us can do—or

avoid doing—to make old age happier and more pleasant
and rewarding for ourselves and for others around us.

1. Keep your place neat, clean, and well organized. Get
   rid of the nonessentials; straighten up what's left. Nothing
   makes one appear more senile than living in the midst of
   mess and old-lady clutter.

2. Keep yourself meticulously groomed and fresh. Wear
   cologne and makeup every day. Wear your good clothes
   —don't save them until they go out of style—so you can
   wear them out. One of the first things people do when
   they start to slip mentally is to neglect their appearance.

3. Walk. Go outside every day and walk. The air, the activity, and the people contact are invigorating. Walk at
   least a mile in good weather, farther if there is time and
   occasion to do so.

4. Walk briskly; swing along; don't plod, amble, or list
   from side to side. Keep your toes pointed straight ahead.
   Keep your head up and your shoulders back. Avoid a
   humped back and a shuffling step as long as you can.

5. When you must use a cane to get around, get a neat
   little walking stick, not one of the ugly brown man-canes
   that make old women look graceless and unfeminine.

6. Sit gracefully. Walk straight up to a chair, then turn
   around and lower yourself into it. Don't lumber up to it
   and plop down as if you were on your very last legs and
   would never be able to rise again.

7. Keep your knees together when you sit. Don't spread
   them apart in typical old-lady fashion. It looks uncouth
   and awkward, especially if you wear dresses and expose
   your garters to every passerby.

8. Don't talk or mutter to yourself in public. We who live
   alone all talk to ourselves in private, and that's all right.
   We keep ourselves company that way. The sound of the
   human voice is a great comfort, even if it's your own.
   But it makes you seem definitely odd to be going down
   the street talking to yourself.

9. Keep your purse neat and organized so you don't fumble in it looking for things. Keep some change in your pocket so you never have to search for the right change when you pay for small purchases or bus fare. It's very annoying to stand behind some old lady who laboriously counts out the right change from two or three coin purses. Have your change ready.

10. Get a second set of keys and attach them to yourself in some way so you are not continually locking yourself out of the apartment.

11. Get a whistling teakettle so you don't let the kettle boil dry every other morning. Stay with the things on the stove. Don't leave them alone.

12. Have a place to put such things as glasses, purse, keys, and scissors, and put them there always, so you don't spend valuable time looking for them.

13. If you can't remember things, write them down. Make lists. Make a list of things you're going to do monthly, weekly, and daily, even if you don't always do them. Make a grocery list, a clothes list, a birthday list, an engagement list, and a list of where you've put things.

14. Don't make a big thing of being forgetful. We are all forgetful. Don't say, "I can't remember things anymore." Say, "For the moment it escapes me," and go on with your conversation as if it didn't matter. It doesn't. The detail you've forgotten is not all that important. No one will notice your forgetfulness if you stop calling attention to it. Don't strain to improve your memory. There are more enjoyable things to do in the time that's left you.

15. Try not to tell the same story to the same people more than once—or twice at the most.

16. If you have nothing of interest to add to a conversation, keep still. Monopolizing conversation is a deadly, old-lady trick. Nothing is more boring than having to put up with someone going on about nothing or telling a dull story that seems to have no ending.

17. Don't talk about your health problems, and don't let others bore you with the details of theirs for any great length of time. Change the subject to something more positive and pleasant.

18. Don't talk about yourself. Don't talk about your past or confide your secrets. Structure the conversation with others so that it centers around them and their interests, not you and yours.

19. Keep an alert look on your face and enthusiasm in your voice. Never answer the phone sounding as if you were half dead.

20. Don't think of yourself as old and sick, even if you are. Visualize yourself as strong and healthy until the end of time—and only temporarily incapacitated.

21. Stay in command of yourself, your life, and your money. Don't let anyone tell you what you should do, certainly not your children. Listen to them patiently and graciously and then do exactly as you please.

22. Don't presume to tell others what they should do, especially not your children. You don't know what they should do—only they know that.

23. Don't act helpless. Don't expect others to be kind or helpful just because you are old. Expect nothing from anybody, and you'll never be disappointed.

24. Don't worry about the future. It may never come. All your plans have been made; you are prepared for all contingencies—illness, death, disability, or a nursing home. Nothing can surprise or shake you now.

25. Don't get in a stew over trivia. What great difference does it make whether the TV repairman comes today or next week?

26. Don't criticize young people out loud. Their hair, their clothes, their attitudes, and their marital status are none of your business. You definitely date yourself and antagonize others with this kind of talk.

27. Try to make some younger friends. At least, try to be-

come acquainted with some young people. Take some classes where you can meet young people and talk with them.

28. Don't keep a lot of money in your purse and don't walk around at night or expose yourself to dangerous situations. Decrepit old ladies are fair game for purse snatchers. A blow on the head can do you no good.

29. Don't keep much money or your valuables in the house either. The fuzzy-headed ones do this, and it's an invitation to criminals. Put your valuables, if you have any, in a safety deposit box.

30. Don't expect everyone to have the same values and standards as you. Theirs may be quite different from yours and perhaps better—at least for them. Don't try to inflict your values and standards and ideas on someone else, especially not on the younger members of your family. When we get old, we tend to become more of whatever we were. Strive to be tolerant and flexible, so you can bend and not break.

31. Work at being charming and considerate of others. Consciously do one thoughtful thing every day for somebody; call up someone, send a card, write a letter, run an errand, or engage someone in conversation and leave them feeling happier with themselves.

32. Keep yourself as healthy as possible with good eating habits and daily exercise. Physical well-being and emotional and mental health are closly related. There is no excuse for not taking exquisite care of yourself now that you have plenty of time.

33. Stay "with it" as long as possible. Read the daily paper from front to back. Read magazines and listen to the news so you know what's going on in the world. Read them at the library if you can't afford to subscribe. Read the best sellers. Have your name put on the list, and the library will mail them to you when they are available— a wonderfully easy way to get reading material.

34. Take up something new every year, something that interests you, something you always wanted to do or learn and never had the time or the opportunity. It doesn't really matter how well you do it, only that you made an attempt. You may surprise yourself! Stay with it for an entire year.

35. Make a conscious effort to keep yourself mentally alert and alive and in contact with the world outside. Take some classes, not for credit but for enjoyment; join anything you feel like joining; do anything you feel like doing.

36. Practice relaxation techniques every day. Sit in the rocking chair and let your body go still and your mind free. Meditate. Visualize yourself as having, being, and doing whatever you want. In your fantasies and in your dreams, you do and you can. Learn to pray passionately and positively.

Then, don't worry about becoming senile. The chances are, you won't. But, if you should, in spite of everything you do, it will probably slip over you while you remain blissfully unaware of its happening. Someone else can worry about it then —not you.

21.

Sewing Secrets for the Older Novice

How to sew beautifully if you are not an expert; how to sew easily, quickly, and painlessly; how to do things your way when you can't do things the expert's way—these are some of the things I have learned since I started sewing. They are things you won't read in the books on sewing because the books are written by experts. These are suggestions for amateurs, for beginning sewers. The experts don't need them.

I like to sew. I really enjoy making my own clothes, but I don't want to spend forever doing it. I want to finish a garment in a day and a half or less and get on to other things. There are many ways to shorten the time you spend on a sewing project and still make a good-looking garment.

Choose Your Fabrics with Care

Some fabrics are easier to sew than others. If not expert, you must learn to select these easy-to-sew, easy-care fabrics, usually in the middle range of weight, firmness, and price. Avoid stripes, plaids, and checks; thin and sleazy materials;

velvet and other pile fabrics; brocades; and those that will fray and ravel unduly at the seam edges. Leave these to experienced dressmakers. Choose double-knit, polyester-cotton, and cotton fabrics. A knowledgeable clerk can help in the selection of material.

Choose Patterns Carefully

Simply styled clothes are easier and quicker to sew and look better on most of us older ones too. Carefully select easy-to-sew patterns with few, rather than many, pieces; avoid those with bound buttonholes, set-in pockets, applied collars and cuffs, lapels, and other tricky, time-consuming construction. These add up to frustration and longer sewing time.

Get the pattern for dresses and blouses in the size nearest your bust measurement, and take the rest of the fitting from there. For pants, get the pattern in the size nearest your hip measurement, not your waist, and work on it until it fits. Make up the pattern first from an old sheet or cheap material, fit it, and then make the adjustments on the paper pattern.

Once you have a classic, basic pattern that fits perfectly, you can use it again and again. Most classic patterns never go out of style. For some figures, fitting takes longer than anything else, so if fitting can be eliminated, you save a great deal of time. I enclose little notes to myself in the pattern envelope concerning the exact amount of material required for *me,* the amount to be allowed and turned under for the hems, and hints on cutting and sewing construction that I won't remember the next time around unless I write them down. Sometimes I can make suggestions to myself for improving the looks of a garment, and the next time I try out these suggestions. A terrific self-help technique, I find.

Time-Savers

I find these inexpensive tools and quick tricks invaluable. They make sewing easy and make your work look as if you had been sewing for years.

A Wrist Pincushion

You can make one for nothing, and it is a great time-saver. Cut out two three-inch circles of material and seam the edges, leaving an opening for stuffing. Turn right side out and stuff it with polyester fill, then whipstitch the opening shut and hand-sew on a little strip of narrow elastic so it can be worn on the wrist. It is much quicker and easier to take pins in and out of a wrist cushion than to fish them from a dish or pick them up from the floor and out of the rug—where most of my pins seem to land when I'm not wearing my pincushion.

A Tailor's Mitt

A dart that shapes a garment to your figure or a curved seam look better when pressed over a tailor's mitt. You can easily make one by cutting two nine-inch-by-five-inch oval pieces of material, seaming them together, turning them right side out, and then stuffing fatly with polyester fill and whipping the top edge shut. If you want to be fancy, make a pretty cover for it, bind the top edge and leave it open so you can take it off and wash it occasionally.

A Ripper

Another thing I've found very helpful is a ripper, an inexpensive little tool you get from the dime store. This saves a lot of time when you goof or when you want to rip out a hem or salvage a zipper from a discarded garment. When you are sewing in the ease in a seam and don't want a tiny, wrinkled pleat to mar the appearance of the seam, you can slide this little tool under the edge to distribute the ease as you sew. It's wonderfully handy.

Cake of Bee's Wax

Another help is bee's wax with which you wax your thread to keep it from snarling when you hand baste, hand sew, or work buttonholes by hand. This eliminates untold frustration.

Have sewing needles in various sizes and a needle threader if you have trouble threading the small ones.

Press-On Interfacing

Another thing to use that makes your simple clothes look great and that saves untold sewing time is press-on interfacing. You want body but not stiffness. A good clerk can recommend the right kind and weight. Take a sample of your material. If you get an inexperienced clerk who doesn't know any more about it than you do, buy the thin kind. It's better to have interfacing too thin than too thick and stiff.

I press interfacing to the garment facing rather than to the garment as some instructions suggest. It works better for me this way. Then, I sew it to the bottom edges of the facing and pink the edges of the facing, rather than hemming the facing under. This eliminates bulk and thickness you don't want. I cut the interfacing a little smaller than the facing piece before I press it on; then I don't have to pull it off when I grade the seams, as the pattern instructions suggest.

Tailor's Chalk

This is used to mark darts and other construction details. Tailor's chalk usually comes in a package of four colors, so you can use a different color for each kind of marking. Lacking this, you can use a pencil—just a very light dot—or a piece of white school chalk. However, these do not erase from the finished garment as easily as does the tailor's chalk.

A Tweezers

This is handy for pulling out little pieces of basting thread that stick up out of the seams. When removing hand basting threads, cut them every three or four inches—don't try to pull the whole thread all at once, or the fabric may be stretched.

Velcro

Another great time-saver that gives a well-finished look to garments and especially to accessories is Velcro—scratchy, sticky strips that fasten things together where you want them and yet pull apart easily. Velcro comes in colored strips that cost about seven cents an inch; you also can get little dots to be machine stitched in place instead of using snap fasteners. I sometimes use it as a fastener for the purses I make, and I always use it on belts. Velcro keeps the back of the belt in place where you want it.

Ballpoint Needles

The right kind and size of machine needle are important too. When sewing double knits and stretchy materials, such as for T-shirts, use what is known as a ballpoint needle. This keeps your straight stitch machine from skipping. When sewing heavy fabrics, use a needle made for heavyweight fabrics. A ballpoint needle can be used most of the time, and you don't need to be changing the needle so often.

Shrinking and Cutting

Before you cut knit material, shrink it by machine washing and drying it. Otherwise, it may not fit after the first washing. Some polyester-cotton fabrics do not need to be washed, only sprinkled heavily, then dried in the dryer. It is the heat that shrinks them.

Press the pattern with a warm iron before you lay it on the material. Lay material with right sides together, if possible, and cut from the wrong side. Then all your pieces will be opposite and you won't wind up with two sleeves for the same arm or two fronts for the same side, a beginner's trick. Put your pins close and cut carefully. A good sharp cutting scissors is a big help. Have it sharpened if it needs it. Do not transfer pattern markings to the garment until you are ready to stitch them. Leave the pattern pinned to the fabric to prevent creases and roll-up.

I find it quicker and easier to cut seam edges straight and to merely clip about ¼ inch into the seam edge at notch symbols. I also clip the seam edges to mark other points I'll be using, such as the shoulder line at the top of the sleeve, the center front or center back of a neckline, the waistline, and so on.

A Quick Way to Mark and Make Darts

Simple patterns have few internal pattern symbols other than those for darts. Working on the padded surface of the ironing board and before unpinning the pattern from the material, I mark each dart symbol with a bit of tailor's chalk in an appropriate color. Then I push a pin straight through the pattern and both layers of fabric at each dot, flop the pattern and material over, and mark the dots with the chalk on the other side where the pins come through. Thus, both sides are easily and quickly marked. Then I stick pins in these markings to pin in the dart. No basting is required, a big time-saver.

Prepare all the darts in all the sections before machine stitching. Then stitch each dart; begin at the wide end, and stitch to the point, then continue stitching down for at least a half inch, catching only one thread of the material. Sew all the darts, then cut the threads. If you have continued stitching after you have sewn off at the point, you do not need to tie the threads.

Press all the darts, first to embed the stitching, then over the press mitt. Slash and trim each dart and turn it to its correct position—vertical darts toward the center of the garment, horizontal ones downward. Thus, the darts are finished in a flash.

Putting In Zippers

If a garment has a zipper, it's easier and faster to apply it to the unassembled garment because there is less material to manipulate. I do it the way the pattern instructions suggest, all except the final stitching. I still cannot sew in a zipper evenly on the machine, even with a zipper foot, so I do it by hand. I backstitch it in with matching thread from the right side, taking very small, even stitches that are practically invisible. I have noticed that some very expensive clothes have zippers put in by hand, so I don't mind doing mine this way.

Seams and Sewing Them

The only reason for hand basting of seams is to ensure that both seam layers move equally as they are being stitched. But you can do the same thing with pins and your hands. (You do this, of course, only if you know the pattern fits.) Working on the ironing board, pin the seam layers together at the notches and at the ends. Match the ends at the seam line, not at the edges. Place pins perpendicular to the seam edges, taking a short nip across the seam line. Then place additional pins about every two inches, making sure they will be on top as you stitch.

Usually, stitch straight seams in a downward direction. For straight seams that are slightly diagonal, as in flared skirts, stitch from the bottom to the top of the garment. The skirt will usually hang better.

Stitch shoulder seams with the eased side against the machine feed.

On crossing seams, I baste a bit just at the crossing and then pin the rest of the way. I place a needle instead of a pin at the junction of the two seams, clip out the bulk if need be by cutting a triangular piece out of the seam allowance, and then baste, to keep the seam allowance from slipping out of position. Clipping out bulk and grading seams should be learned early in your sewing career because this gives clothes a well-finished look.

Some curved seams can be handled like straight seams. If a seam has a slight curve, such as a side seam of a dress, skirt, or pants from hip to waist, you can pin instead of baste. But a novice should baste other curved seams after stay stitching and clipping the edges as suggested in the pattern instructions.

Sleeves and How to Do Them

The way your set-in sleeves look is the criterion of your sewing skill, the detail that makes a simple garment look sharp. (There isn't much else you can do wrong.) The seam line must hit the exact edge of the shoulder without a wrinkle, and there must be ease in the back so you can move your arm comfortably without any pull.

What follows is an amateur's way of putting in a good-looking sleeve, not the way the pattern instructions suggest. In addition to slashing the single and double notches in the seam line, mark three other points to enable you to distribute the ease properly—the top of the sleeve that matches the shoulder seam, the dot in the front, and the dot in the back. Mark by clipping ¼ inch into the seam allowance of both the sleeve and the armhole at these points.

Put ease stitches in the sleeve, starting ½ inch below the top-of-the-sleeve mark and ending at the last notch near the bottom of the sleeve. Loosen the tension and lengthen the stitch on the machine before stitching, and then stitch ⅝ inch from the edge with the right side up. Some pattern instructions tell you to put in two rows of stitching, but I get better results with only one. Now stitch from the other bottom notch to within ½ inch of the top of the sleeve.

Turn the garment wrong side out and the sleeve right side out. From underneath, bring the top of the sleeve into the armhole and pin it in six places: at the underarm seam; at the shoulder; at the front notch; at the back notch; and at the two dot points. Place these pins on the seam line. Pull the gathering thread on one side, easing the sleeve cap to the shoulder mark. Pull the thread on the other side, easing the sleeve to the shoulder mark. Distribute the ease equally with your fingers. You don't want any fullness in the top inch of the sleeve. If there is too much fullness, I shrink out some of it with the tip of the steam iron. It isn't always necessary to do this—it depends on the pattern.

A novice should now baste the sleeve in by hand, taking a ⅝-inch seam, and then try on the garment to see that the sleeve fits perfectly. If it doesn't, you'll have to take the whole thing apart and make adjustments by trimming the armhole just a tiny bit where it needs it.

When the basted-in sleeve suits you, machine stitch it on the sleeve side, with the sleeve against the presser foot and the seam edge to the right of the needle; start at the underarm seam allowance and stitch just inside the ease stitching. Overlap the stitching across the underarm seam allowance.

I stitch the seam twice, the second time slightly outside the seam line, and then trim both seam allowances outside the last stitching, usually pinking the material. Press the stitching lightly from the inside, then fingerpress the seam down toward the sleeve bottom. Next, insert a rolled towel and lightly press the seam down, laying the tip of the iron lightly on the seam only at the top of the sleeve.

A Quick Way with Necks

Instead of facing a plain neck, it's much easier and quicker to put on a binding. I like the bound look better anyway. There are several ways to handle bindings, and each method results in a slightly different look. You can use a double bias binding or a single bias binding. Experiment with various widths and types of strips until you find the one that best suits you and the particular garment. Then trim out the neckline edge of the garment so the finished edge of the binding will extend to the pattern seam line; otherwise, the neck will not fit perfectly.

Cut the binding on the true bias. Measure and be accurate in keeping the width even. Try to cut sufficient binding for the neckline in one piece so that you don't have to join the strips, thus eliminating a seam.

Bindings can be used in other places, instead of facings —for example, on armholes, sleeve ends, and hemlines. They make a neat, distinctive finish.

Quick Armhole Finishes

When making sleeveless jackets to wear with pants, I put a double bias facing strip around the armholes instead of making the armhole facings shown in the pattern. Neither my machine nor I top stitch very well, but I like to hand sew; so I usually attach the facing strip by hand. First I backstitch it flat to the underside of the garment, taking the stitches about ½ inch from the edge and working from the right side. Then, I hand sew the wider front facings about ½ inch from the edge to match. This is much easier than fussing about with facing, interfacing, basting, turning, and pressing, and it gives the garment a smart, hand-finished look. Many expensive coats and suits are hand-finished this way. (Occasionally I look-shop among the very expensive clothes, and I note how they are seamed, interfaced, hemmed and finished.)

Making a Quick Hem

A skimpy hem, poorly put in, makes any garment look cheap. You should not be able to see a hem unless the fabric is very sheer. Many moderately priced garments have poorly done hems, as do some of the expensive ones. When cutting a skirt and pants, be sure to allow enough material to turn up an ample hem, and let the garment hang on a hanger overnight before pinning up a hem. If a skirt has been properly fitted, it will hang evenly, and it will not be necessary to have anyone measure where the hem should be placed. Pin the hem and then hand baste it near the fold and again at the top, taking out the pins. Try on the garment to see that it hangs perfectly, and then measure the hem width evenly and cut off the excess. On knits, I invisibly stitch the raw edges in place without any finish at all. If the hem flares too much, you should narrow it a bit, and it may require ease stitching to control the edge. I put the ease in by hand, too, with a running stitch that I can gather slightly as I make the blind hemstitching. Then I press the fullness out. When giving the hem a final pressing, press only the fold of the hem. These quick, hand-done hems look smooth and perfect.

Finishing Seams

Many present-day materials are firm enough so that the seam edges need no finishing unless they are going to show, as in an unlined jacket. Most can simply be pinked. I hand-pink with my cutting scissors, cutting out little chunks before I press the seams open, thus halving the time it takes. Denim will ravel unless the seams are finished, and flat, double-sewn seams as in bought jeans take considerable time. I cut the seams on denim wider than the pattern, then machine stitch close to the edge, turn that edge under, and stitch again.

22.

A Mini Course in Make-Do Decorating

If you want to try to tackle some repair jobs yourself—and occasionally you may have to—there are a number of books available that will show and tell you exactly what to do. If you are still in your own home, you can certainly save a lot of money and a lot of frustration by taking care of many of the repairs yourself. Every woman should be able to make repairs, especially minor ones, but many of us older ones are totally ignorant in this area, which makes us more dependent on others than we should be.

Although no book can anticipate every problem, some are more successful than others—and some are easier for the novice to understand. *The Reader's Digest Complete Do-It-Yourself Manual* is very complete, and also very big. There is a section called "Women's Guide to Household Emergencies," which may be helpful. I don't recommend that you buy this book, but I do recommend that you ask for it at the library and browse through it; then you will know the kind of information and help it can provide if and when you need it. It's well organized and covers an enormous number of subjects, probably more than most of us want to know about.

The Feminine Fix-It Handbook by K. B. Ward, published by Grossett and Dunlap, costs only $1.95 in paperback and is written specifically for women. Ward assumes, probably rightly, that her reader knows nothing about tools and repairing, and she immediately proceeds to enlighten her, telling how to fix a leaky faucet and the lamp that won't light, and what to do about peeling paint and cracked windowpanes and doors that drag. She also tells how to paint a ceiling, paper a room, hang a shelf on the wall, lay a tile floor, panel a room, and repair and refinish furniture. A careful reading of this book, followed by some practice with book in hand, should enable any woman to maintain her apartment or house practically single-handed. Ward also tells when to call for help.

Reading the directions may make some tasks such as painting and wallpapering seem more difficult and involved than they really are. However, if an older woman has never painted a ceiling or papered a room, I do not recommend that she attempt these chores. She can paper an alcove or paint a wall, but she should probably not undertake a complete interior decorating job by herself if she doesn't know what she is getting into. If you are past seventy, I have only one word of advice: Don't. Climbing around on a ladder can lead to broken bones. Get your family or young friends to help with these redecorating chores.

Refinishing, Antiquing, Painting, and Decorating Furniture

Refinishing furniture is also time-consuming, back-breaking work. To do a good job requires more skill and strength than most of us possess. You must spend hours repairing, filling, sanding, staining, and waxing, which an inexperienced worker does not know how to do well. If you have a piece that is a real "find," you may want to take a class in refinishing and devote yourself to it for a few months.

However, if you have a collection of furniture from someone's attic or the second-hand store, or nondescript furniture of your own that has seen better days, you don't have to live with it. There are ways of refurbishing and renovating this furniture to make it look respectable without going to all the work of actually refinishing it.

In my quest for something simple that I could do, I discovered antiquing. I found that I could do an adequate job of it, and that old, ugly furniture could be transformed with a minimum of time and effort. The purpose of antiquing is to make furniture look antique, so any holes, dents, and gouges contribute to the authenticity of the piece.

I used the Sherwin-Williams antiquing products, and I started with a kit. However, if you have more than a piece or two to do, it will pay to buy the products in larger sizes. I personally think their Cherrywood finish does more for old, battered furniture than any other, although they have many other colors. This finish requires three coats: the primary base coat, a color base called Heirloom, and a third color-glaze coat called Delft. The primary coat costs about $2.00 a pint; the other coats cost $2.65 for ½ pint and come only in these size cans, but they go a long way.

The directions that come with the kit are quite explicit. However, I did not spend hours preparing and sanding each piece as the directions suggest. If you did this, you would have a smoother, somewhat more beautiful piece, I suppose, but it would take hours and more perseverance and stamina than I possess. Since most of the pieces you will do are probably rather old-fashioned and battered, the rougher finish is fine. First, you remove the hardware, then give the piece a going-over with a turpentined rag, and sand it for ten or fifteen minutes or until fatigued. There is no need to remove the old finish as the undercoat will completely cover it.

The first base coat is then applied with a brush; it dries in about an hour, and the second coat, Heirloom, is applied, brushed out, and streaked a bit with the brush. I no longer wipe this second coat as the directions say to do. This should be permitted to dry for at least twenty-four hours, and then the third coat, called Delft, is applied and allowed to dry for twenty minutes or so and then judiciously wiped with a soft, lint-free rag and streaked with a brush. It is the wiping of this third coat that determines how the piece will look. The secret is to know how much of the second and third coats to streak and wipe off, and to do it with finesse. You can do it to imitate woodgrain or make interesting swoops and swirls. This comes with a bit of practice. If you are not satisfied with your first attempt, you can wipe it off and start over. It may be a good idea to practice a bit on an old piece of board and experiment a little to get the effect you want, to see what you can do.

When the piece is thoroughly dry, it is given a coat of varnish or wax. Wax is easier to apply and less time consuming. To apply varnish well, you have to know how. I simply spray with Johnson's Pledge when the piece is thoroughly dry and buff to a nice, soft glow.

The Sherwin-Williams products can be cleaned up with water, and they come in a variety of finishes with luscious-sounding names such as Harvest Yellow, Florentine Gold, Butternut, Mediterranean Olive, Brittany Blue, and Spanish Red. The color samples you look at in the store will be approximate. The actual color effect will depend somewhat upon glaze application and wiping techniques. A friend and I did her bedroom furniture in Victorian White and a dining table and chairs in Spanish Red; they both came out looking quite elegant.

Painting Furniture

If you don't want to go to the work of antiquing, you can paint your old, nondescript furniture and make it match. Buy a good brand of quick-dry enamel. Lightly sand the old finish to rough it up, and then paint after dusting it well. One coat of a dark color may suffice. If you are painting a piece a lighter color, two or three coats may be necessary. Rough up with sandpaper between coats and wipe thoroughly to remove the dust.

A friend and I painted a roomful of cast-off furniture with

black enamel, made bright cushions for the chairs, covered the divan, and made curtains from the same material. The room looked very nice.

If you have a piece of unpainted furniture you want to do, it may pay you to apply a primer-and-sealer coat before painting. Or, if there are knots in the wood, they should be painted with one part shellac and one part denatured alcohol. This will keep the knots from striking through the enamel.

You may want to beautify a piece by adding a stencil design. These designs can be as intricate or as simple as you wish—or paint on a decoration freehand. A good job of painting thus decorated transforms an inexpensive piece of furniture into a delightful conversation piece. If you don't know how to stencil, go to the library and get a book. You can find patterns for designs also. Thus, you put a rich look into your place for pennies. The look you achieve is limited only by imagination, not your pocketbook.

Decorating with Mosaic Tile

If you have a piece of furniture with a recessed top that is somewhat the worse for wear, you can decorate it with mosaic tile. To tile a small piece of furniture such as an old table, you will need to get tile in foot-square sections and a supply of grout. The clerk will try to sell you glue with which to lay the tile and wax to finish it, but these are not really necessary.

Tile comes in a variety of colors, shapes, and sizes, and the grout comes in a variety of colors. I break the tile apart and glue it down with Elmer's glue in a pleasing hit-and-miss pattern or design. When this is dry, mix the grout with water and apply it to the cracks. Keep working the grout in and pressing it with your fingers. When it has hardened slightly, wipe the piece with a damp sponge and polish with your fingers. Let dry a bit more and polish with a paper towel. In a day or two spray it with Johnson's Pledge and polish it.

Decorating with Fabric

Even if you sew only a little, you can make drapes, curtains, slipcovers, bedspreads, cushions, and all kinds of accessories for your house for very little.

Getting Ideas

To get ideas for the things you can do, go to the library and get some books on interior decorating and decorating with fabric. Many of the projects described in the books will be too expensive for poor old women, and some of the things described require more sewing skill than most of us presently possess. However, these books will give you ideas for the many ways you can create beauty in your own little apartment or house. The authors describe the making of all kinds of curtains, drapes, cushions, bedspreads, wall hangings, lamp shades, tablecloths, and headboards—and some things most of us would never think of making.

Patterns and Information

The pattern companies—Simplicity, McCall's, Butterick, and others—feature patterns for café curtains, bedspreads, tablecloths, and various accessories for the house. A look through these pattern books will also give you ideas, and you can buy the pattern or carry the idea home in your head and cut your own pattern. It's cheaper, of course, to cut your own. Anyone who can measure with a yardstick and tape measure can learn to cut her own.

You will also find in the fabric and needlework departments booklets that tell you how to make drapes and curtains of all kinds, slipcovers, bedspreads, and other things you might need to beautify your surroundings. The booklets usually cost about a dollar, and they explain exactly how to proceed.

Inexpensive Fabric—Sheets

The novice will probably hesitate to cut into expensive fabrics. Dexterity, confidence, and skill come with practice, and most of us will feel more comfortable working with inexpensive fabrics. Where do you find them?

The most inexpensive fabric you can use for decorating is sheets. Today's sheets come in all colors and patterns from basic white to black, from floral patterns to jungle prints, and everything in between. If you use the less expensive sheets, the cost is less than a dollar a yard. Where else can you find decorating fabric for that price?

Sheets can be used for almost anything—curtains, drapes, bedspreads, cushions, slipcovers, shower curtains, closet accessories, placemats, tablecloths, hot-pot holders, appliance covers, and ironing board covers. Sheets are sturdy and machine washable and do not need ironing, and many times the prehemmed and selvage edges can be taken advantage of to eliminate a lot of sewing.

Recently, the magazines have been featuring sheets in some very posh projects, too expensive and too much work for most of us, but there are many simpler projects you can undertake for a start. I used sheets in my apartment because I had them on hand, having bought them on sale for a song several years previously.

Bedspread

I made everything in the bedroom match by putting a fitted sheet and top sheet on the bed and then making a bedspread from another top sheet. I pinned up a triangular corner on the bottom of the spread at the foot of the bed and whipstitched it in place, then sewed fringe, which I made from rug yarn, around the edges. A matching pillowcase covered the pillow, which was propped against the wall, facilitating bed making. This is a very practical spread, colorful and easily laundered.

Comforter with Dust Ruffle

If you should be so fortunate as to have a down coverlet or other warm comforter, it can be enclosed between two matching sheets and used with a dust ruffle that hangs to the floor, so that no other spread is necessary. An easy way to make the dust ruffle is to cut strips the width you need, piece

them to a length double the distance around the bed, finish
the bottom, hem the top edge, run cording or twine though the
top hem, and gather it to fit. Then pin it to the mattress with
small safety pins. The comforter comes down over it to con-
ceal the pins.

Drapes

One sheet will usually make side drapes for a window with
a glass curtain between. It is not always necessary to rehem
the top or the side that goes against the window frame. I
tore the sheet in two lengthwise, ran a row of machine stitching down the center of the top hems to make the headings,
and then hemmed the sides that went against the glass curtain.
The glass curtain and side drapes can go on the same curtain
rod.

For pull drapes, I used two sheets crosswise, hemmed the
sides that were to form the top of the drapes and sewed on
pinch-pleat tape, and then inserted the hardware to make the
pleats. This is a very easy way to make drapes—anyone can
do it, even if you've never tried to make drapes before. You
get the tape and hardware at the drapery department of almost
any store. Directions for making them come with the tape.

I found it more satisfactory to measure up the hems of the
curtains and drapes after I had hung them, the ways some
people take a dress hem by measuring up from the floor with
a yardstick. In less expensive sheets, the threads may not be
exactly horizontal and vertical, and if you tear the bottom edge
and hem it before you put up the curtain, it won't necessarily
hang straight. Don't wash the sheets before you make curtains
and drapes; inexpensive sheets are prettier and have more of
a soil-resistant finish before they are washed.

Shower Curtain

I made a shower curtain for the bathroom out of a sheet
cut crosswise, using an inexpensive white liner I bought from
the dime store. Cut the sheet the same size as the liner, make

tiny holes in the top with an ice pick or some other sharp instrument, and insert the hooks through the liner and hemmed top of the curtain.

Closet Accessories

I made these accessories from the pieces I cut off the bottoms of the sheets when making curtains. I made scalloped shelf edgings for closets, a purse hanger, garment protectors, a laundry bag, and a closet storage bag with hanging shelves. I bought an old closet storage bag at a garage sale, cut the material off to use as a pattern, used the same shelves and zipper, and recovered the frame with fresh, bright sheet material. I could have made one from wire coat hangers, cardboard, and twine, but it would have been more work.

Hat and Storage Boxes

Boxes of all kinds can be covered with leftover material. Measure the box and seam the material to fit it, leaving extra length to paste down at the top and at the bottom of the box. Paste with ordinary school paste bought at the dime store, which will not strike through the material. Lids are similarly covered, with the corners of the material slashed and the edges of the material turned to the inside.

The Way to a Neat Closet

Pattern companies show patterns for making all kinds of closet accessories—shoe bags, covered hangers, purse hangers, garment protectors, and laundry bags, as well as various kinds of shelf edgings. With a bit of ingenuity, you can learn to cut your own patterns. A neat, well-organized, good-looking closet can be easily achieved if you sew just a bit.

Covering an Ironing Board and Sleeve Board

Pieces left over from other projects will cover an ironing board and sleeve board. To make an ironing board cover, draw an outline of the ironing board on a piece of wrapping paper or newspapers pasted together, allow six or seven inches extra all around, and cut the material to this dimension. Make a ¾-inch hem around the entire piece, leaving a small, unsewed place at the large end for inserting the cord. Thread heavy wrapping cord into the hem with a bodkin or safety pin, then pull it up to fit the board and tie. If the cover does not stay taut underneath, thread cord through a big darning needle and fasten the cover securely by cross sewing on the underside every 8 inches or so. Likewise, make a cover for the sleeve board, threading ¼-inch elastic through the hem.

Studio Couch Cover

Sheets make inexpensive couch covers. Rip apart the old cover and use it for a pattern. Or, cut your own after reading directions for doing so in one of the booklets purchased at a sewing center.

Covering a Bolster or Cushion

To cover a bolster or a foam cushion for a chair, cut bottom and top pieces to fit it, cut side strips to fit, buy contrasting cording—this is much easier than making your own—and machine-baste it in place. Then, sew the cover, leaving the back seam open. Place the cover over the bolster or cushion and whipstitch it shut. You can insert a zipper if you wish, but it is easier not to. The secret of good-looking covers is making them tight. Allow a ½-inch seam when measuring and cutting the pieces. You will need a cording foot attachment for your sewing machine, but these are not expensive.

Floor-Length Tablecloth for a Round Table

Measure the distance from the floor across the table and down to the floor on the other side and cut a circle of this diameter. Edge it with ball fringe. If the table is a large one, you may need a wide sheet to avoid seaming. Measure before you buy, however, as the larger sheets are more expensive.

Using Coordinated Sheets for Decorating

You can now buy coordinated sheets. A friend and I decorated her apartment by using sheets in a shade of blue that she liked. We bought sheets that were plain, striped, or had a large flower print, all in the same lovely shade of blue, to make a couch cover, curtains, cushions, chair seats, and a floor-length tablecloth to cover her round fiberboard table. Even though poor, you do not need to live with ugliness. Ingenuity and time can take the place of money.

Other Inexpensive Materials

You may want to consider burlap and unbleached muslin. Get the permanent press muslin that does not require ironing, but do not shop for it in the drapery department, where it will probably be expensive. Get it in the regular piece-goods section, where you may find it for a dollar a yard or a little more.

Burlap, in natural or in colors, with cross-stitch borders makes attractive, rustic-looking curtains that let the light through. Put them on rings on interesting-looking rods. They look nice and can be pulled easily across windows and doors. Big cross-stitch on burlap makes attractive, decorative cushions and wall hangings. You can also pull heavy yarn through burlap to make decorative finishes.

Burlap, unbleached muslin, macrame wall hangings, jute, and hanging plants add up to a natural look that is popular these days and inexpensive if you do it yourself.

Scraps

Of course, the most inexpensive material of all is scraps. Anyone who sews has scraps. Some people who sew but do not have the time or inclination to use their scraps will sometimes give them to you if you hint subtly. You can also buy them at garage sales. When you use scraps for decorating, you will probably have to buy only a yard or two of new material to tie your color scheme together. Scraps can be pieced into cushions, bedspreads, tablecloths, wall hangings, or chair covers—ideal projects for old ladies who like to create something gay and colorful but haven't much money to spend.

Rugs and Floors

You can make a small hooked, braided, or crocheted rug. The first attempt should be a small one, so that if you don't enjoy this particular type of rug making, you don't have a lot of material on hand. A small rug is quickly finished.

To make a small crocheted rug for the bathroom or a small kitchen rug to stand on while you are at the sink, get two skeins of rug yarn in two colors, and, using a single crochet stitch, crochet a striped rug of the size you need.

A rectangular rug is the easiest to make. Chain the length you want, turn, and single crochet. Keep turning and single crocheting until the strip is the width you want.

Join the other color and likewise crochet a strip the same width. Continue until the rug is the width you want. Attach fringe at the ends by looping and tying two or three strands of cut yarn through the end stitches.

You can also make oval or round crocheted rugs but you must be a bit more skilled to make them lie flat.

A Hooked Rug

You can make a small hooked rug from a kit that you buy. Of course, these are more expensive than those you design yourself, but by working first with a kit, you learn how to do it. The hooked rugs made from kits are pretty.

A Braided Rug

To make a braided rug, you should have a device that attaches to your scissors and enables you to cut a strip the width you want. There are also devices that slip onto the strips and turn the raw edges inside as you braid. The devices with a book of instructions for making braided rugs can be purchased from a hobby or needlework shop.

However, if you tear your material and press or sew it so that the raw edges are on the inside, you won't need the devices or directions, although this pressing or sewing takes longer. You will, perhaps, need a book from the library on making braided rugs.

I made my first very easy and very inexpensive braided rug for a friend's bathroom by tearing some old white sheets into strips, pressing the raw edges inward, braiding the strips, and sewing the braid in an oval shape. It cost nothing and looked quite nice in her old-fashioned bathroom with a painted floor and a tub with claw feet.

The advantage of making your own rugs is that you can tailor them to fit your space and color scheme. If you can use scraps and discarded materials, they cost nothing at all.

Cutting and Laying a Bathroom Carpet

If your bathroom floor is bad, a plushy wall-to-wall carpet will make it look quite elegant, and it is about the easiest and most inexpensive thing you can do. If the space to be covered is small, the cost is not exorbitant, and the carpeting can be washed as needed in an ordinary washing machine. A rug for a larger area will cost more and be difficult to wash— you will probably have to take it to the laundromat—so consider doing something else with a bad floor in a large bathroom.

Measure the bathroom carefully to get the amount of carpeting needed. Then, paste newspaper or wrapping paper together, lay it on the floor, and cut the paper until it fits to perfection. Use this pattern to cut the rug with an ordinary scissors.

Fitting and cutting the paper pattern enables you to do a sharp-looking job of cutting and laying the carpeting in place. A large piece of paper sometimes comes with the carpeting.

Loose-Laying a Carpet

Sometimes, cleaning the carpet or rug does not remove the spots and stains, or it is worn and ugly. One thing you can do is to cover it up with other carpeting. If you intend to be in a place for a time, but not forever, cutting and loose-laying an inexpensive carpeting in the color and texture of your choice over the one already there makes a room look fresh and inviting. When you leave, you can take it with you and hope that it can be cut to fit it in your new place. In the meantime, it will lie satisfactorily over the soiled and worn carpeting that came with the place.

Refinishing a Floor

Sometimes you can remove the old carpeting and paint, refinish, or antique a floor, and then get a small area rug or two. Two smaller rugs are usually less expensive than one larger one, although a larger rug will cover a large expanse of ugly floor and may be a solution to your problem.

When painting a floor, finish with several coats of clear floor varnish.

You can also get carpeting with adhesive backing that you stick down in squares. It comes in a variety of patterns and colors, and in shag, tufted, and matte.

Laying a Tile Floor

If you are considering redoing a floor, go to a tile dealer and note the infinite variety of handsome patterns available. You *can* lay a tile floor, in spite of what your son-in-law may say. I recommend that you use only the self-stick tile. Then you won't need to bother with spreading the adhesive, which can be a great mess. The self-stick tiles have a removable paper backing that protects the adhesive. All you have to do is pull it off and lay them according to the directions that come with the tile, putting the center tile in the exact center of the floor and laying in the sequence suggested.

Lamps

You can occasionally find inexpensive lamps, costing not more than three or four dollars, at the dime store or second-hand store. Or, you can make your own from bottles, jars, or jugs that you have on hand. I made a kitchen lamp from a cider jug, and a pair of lamps for a friend from some green glass prune-juice bottles. You can get the makings for a lamp at a hardware store. A knowledgeable clerk can tell you what you need and what to do.

If you need more help than the clerk can give you, get a book from the library on making lamps. Craft magazines and women's magazines also have occasional articles on how to make unusual lamps and lighting fixtures from tin cans, styrofoam cups, foil plates, and other inexpensive materials.

Lamp Shades

Old, soiled lamp shades can be covered with material or paper. When covering a shade with paper, roll the shade over the paper, marking at both the top and bottom edges with a pencil as you roll. Cut out the paper and glue it in place over the old or inexpensive shade.

Material can also be pasted in place, with the raw edges concealed at the top and bottom with fringe, braid, or a length of chain you crochet yourself from contrasting rug yarn or leftover pieces of knitting yarn.

When covering a straight or slightly flared shade, it's easier to measure from the top to the bottom of the shade and cut a strip of material, slightly slanted as need be, to these dimensions. Allow ¼ inch for the seams, and seam the material on a sewing machine. This tube is then pulled down over the shade to fit tautly. Again, the raw edges can be covered with fringe, braid, or crocheted chain lightly glued to the shade with ordinary white glue.

A skimpy shade can be lengthened with a strip of straight or ball fringe glued to the bottom. Or, you can crochet a chain from rug yarn and then pull more yarn evenly through the chain with a crochet hook, leaving the ends of the yarn looped. When trimmed evenly, it makes a close fringe. This is a good way to use up scraps of leftover yarn, and it costs nothing.

Pictures, Pillows, and Plants

Good pitcures and frames are expensive; so you can make your own or buy inexpensive ones. You can buy inexpensive reproductions of your favorite paintings and then frame them yourself, have them framed, or buy a frame that fits. You can often buy a simple, inexpensive frame from the dime store to fit your picture. If you can't find a frame to fit exactly, get a slightly larger size and mat the picture with a big piece of drawing paper.

A picture that you like cut from an old calendar and put in a dime store frame costs almost nothing.

The dime store is also the place for poor people to buy mirrors.

Mirrors are usually good in small rooms—they make them appear larger. A friend of mine bought several small, darkly framed mirrors from the dime store and mounted them behind her divan. They looked quite nice, and they cost only a fraction of what a large, solid plate-glass mirror would have cost.

A hand-embroidered sampler can add a touch of individuality to a room. Samplers can be made from a kit that comes complete with yarn, needle, and instructions. A frame to fit can usually be ordered with the kit. However, if you are at all adept, you can design and make your own samplers, wall hangings, and other things to decorate your walls. A look through the magazines and needlecraft books will give you ideas, as will a visit to an arts and crafts show. I always carry a notebook with me, and I sketch and make notes of ideas that appeal to me and that I think I might be able to duplicate or adapt. You can use felt in reverse appliqué, make a string sculpture with string or gift wrap, make a macrame hanging, or frame a beautiful fabric to put on your wall. Or, you might take a course in painting and fill your place with your own original art.

Pillows

A few decorative pillows and cushions scattered about make a couch or corner look cozy and inviting. However, luxurious, beautifully made pillows are extremely expensive. But you can make your own for almost nothing if you use scraps. You can make beautifully pieced and quilted pillows, appliquéd pillows, or tailored pillows; you can also make needlepoint pillows or crewel embroidered pillows. Look in the decorator shops for the kinds of pillows you want, then go home and duplicate them.

You do not need a pillow form for many of these pillows. By stuffing your pillow with polyester fill, which you can get at the dime store, you will have fat, soft, washable pillows if the material from which they are made is washable. Otherwise, you must have them dry cleaned.

You can buy kits to make embroidered pillows, or you can design your own. If you cannot draw your own embroidery design, buy a transfer pattern and stamp your material. You'll find this is much cheaper than buying a kit. Instead of buying braid or fringe to finish a pillow, you can chain a piece of yarn and whipstitch it over the seam edges. This gives a nice finish to some pillows. Important-looking tassels for the corners of a pillow can easily be made from left-over yarn and attached to the corners when you seam the pillow front to the back. To make tassels, wind yarn around a piece of cardboard of the size desired, then cut one end of the yarn and tie the other end tightly with a length of yarn, leaving ends for joining to the corners. Finally, wrap more yarn tightly around it to make the tassel.

If you want a very quick embroidered pillow, get some burlap, mark it into squares, and cross-stitch it with leftover yarn. Make the center square first, and continue cross-stitching each set of squares around the center in a different color. In an hour you'll have the pillow top finished.

To make a no-cost patchwork pillow top, cut scraps in little squares and piece them. Cut a backing to the size you need, seam it, turn it right side out, and stuff. Put a double ruffle around the edge if you wish.

Plants

Nothing makes a room look more luxurious than an assortment of beautiful, green, growing plants scattered about, massed against a wall or window, or serving as a room divider. Plants bring life and color to any room.

If you insist on buying those big, beautiful, luxuriant plants at the florist and garden shops, you will spend a fortune. But you can start small and grow your own plants for pennies. In fact, it's more fun this way, and, in time and with care, these little plants become large and dramatic foliage.

A green thumb is nothing more than a bit of knowledge and a lot of patience. To grow and thrive, plants need proper soil, light, food, water, and drainage. Without these no plant will thrive, and a puny, drooping, untidy plant is a depressing sight.

If you don't know anything about growing plants, perhaps you can get a green-thumbed friend to start you off with a few slips from her garden. Lacking a friend with plants, you can do your own thing quite inexpensively.

Go to a dime store or garden shop and get a few ordinary clay pots—or pick up discards from the garbage or at garage sales. Clay pots with a hole in the bottom for drainage are the best kind. If you have big, pretty pots or hanging baskets you want to use, set the clay pots inside. If you must use containers with no holes in their bottoms, put several layers of pebbles and some charcoal in the bottom for drainage. Drainage is absolutely essential.

If you don't like the looks of the clay pots, make some

plant pot covers from fabric that matches your room decor. These are attractive and the cheapest kind of pot covers.

Also from the garden shop, get a sack of potting soil. Don't try to use ordinary garden dirt. Potting soil is sterile and the right mix for most growing plants. This may be a bit more expensive than mixing your own, but it's easier, cleaner, and quicker.

Then, buy some starting plants in little pots. Unfortunately, these will cost you more than a dollar apiece. In my opinion, the plants that are easiest for the amateur to grow and that make a nice beginning are ivy, philodendron, wandering Jew, and geraniums. Scoop them out of their plastic pots and set them in the potting soil in the clay pot, pressing the soil down firmly around the roots, and water judiciously. If you want a big, dramatic plant in a hurry, set several of the little starting plants in a big container.

More plants are killed from overwatering than underwatering. Water most plants only when the top of the soil feels rather dry to the touch. Water in a quantity so that water runs out the bottom hole. Let the plant drain thoroughly before replacing the pot in its saucer or lid. Plants should be watered with water at room temperature which you have drawn from the tap and let set overnight.

In order to thrive, foliage plants need at least six hours a day of direct, bright light such as sunlight filtering through a curtain. Flowering plants need from two to four hours of direct sun—they won't produce flowers properly unless they have sun.

If you place the plants where they get little or no direct light, you must have a grow light which you can get at a garden shop or dime store. The most inexpensive kind is a grow light bulb that you screw into an ordinary lamp. Ideally, it should be hung above your plants at a distance of several feet or slightly more.

Once you have the plants started, get a little envelope of

plant food to fertilize your plants every two or three weeks by putting this powder in their water, but use only about half as much fertilizer as the directions call for.

To keep the leaves of your plants dust free and pretty, mist them in the morning by spraying them with some of the settled water put in a spray bottle. If the air in your room is very dry in the winter time, boil a kettle of water on the stove. Raising the humidity level of your room is good for you as well as for your plants. Keep the plants clean and well-groomed, pick off the dead leaves, and keep the pot edges clean.

When a plant gets too big for its starting pot, repot it into a bigger one. When repotting ivy or philodendron, you may want to set a pole or stick firmly into the soil for the bigger plant to vine around. The wandering Jew is a rapid grower, and the dropping stems make it an ideal hanging plant. If you have a big container, get a full planting for the container at the beginning. In a few months you should have a big, beautiful plant.

Growing Greenery from Vegetables

If you want some greenery in your house and have no money at all to spend on plants, you can put an ordinary sweet potato in water and watch the leaves grow from the top. You can also plant a carrot in a pot of soil, water it well, and greenery will appear at the top; in six to eight weeks, if you are lucky, you will also have some flowers that resemble Queen Anne's lace.

Grow Your Garbage

The seed of an avocado can be used to start an attractive house plant. Choose a large avocado. You may want to try several seeds to get at least one that will grow. Remove the seed from the avocado and wash it thoroughly in warm water. Stick three toothpicks a little way into the seed and suspend it half in and half out of a glass; the broad end goes down and the pointed end sticks up. Put enough water in the glass to cover about an inch of the base of the seed.

Check the container daily to be sure the water is maintained at the correct level. A bit of patience is required at this point. It may take six weeks or longer before the seed cracks and roots begin to poke through the bottom. The seed can be potted at this time, but you may also leave it in the water until a sprout shoots up from the top. This will take another four to six weeks, but after that the growth of the plant will be rapid.

Plant the sprouted seed in a large pot with a drainage hole. Set the seed in potting soil so that about one-third of it remains above the soil. Soak it thoroughly with water, but then let it dry out before watering again. Set in the direct sunlight if you have sun.

If you want a bushy, compact plant, prune it to three inches when it gets about five inches high. I can never bring myself to do this, and so I let the plant grow, setting the pot on the floor and staking my tree to encourage it to grow straight and tall. Four months after you have planted the seed in the pot, you should have a plant from three to four feet high, all for the price of an avocado.

If you have direct, bright light, you can also play with lemon seeds, orange seeds, and apple seeds, covering these tiny seeds with only a fraction of an inch of soil. Why spend money buying plants when you can plant vegetables and your own garbage for nothing?

Index